CAMPAIGN 331

SMOLENSK 1943

The Red Army's Relentless Advance

ROBERT FORCZYK

ILLUSTRATED BY ADAM HOOK
Series editor Marcus Cowper

Osprey Publishing
c/o Bloomsbury Publishing Plc
PO Box 883, Oxford, OX1 9PL, UK
Or
c/o Bloomsbury Publishing Inc.
1385 Broadway, 5th Floor, New York, NY 10018, USA
Email: info@ospreypublishing.com

www.ospreypublishing.com

OSPREY is a trademark of Osprey Publishing Ltd, a division of Bloomsbury
Publishing Plc.

First published in Great Britain in 2019

A CIP catalogue record for this book is available from the British Library.

ISBN: PB: 978 1 4728 3074 6
           ePub: 978 1 4728 3073 9
           ePDF: 978 1 4728 3075 3
           XML: 978 1 4728 3076 0

19 20 21 22 23 10 9 8 7 6 5 4 3 2 1

Index by Fionbar Lyons
Typeset in Myriad Pro and Sabon
Maps by Bounford.com
3D BEVs by The Black Spot
Page layouts by PDQ Digital Media Solutions, Bungay, UK
Printed in China through World Print Ltd.

Artist's note

Readers may care to note that the original paintings from which the colour
plates in this book were prepared are available for private sale. All
reproduction copyright whatsoever is retained by the Publishers. All
enquiries should be addressed to:

Scorpio, 158 Mill Road, Hailsham, East Sussex BN27 2SH, UK

The Publishers regret that they can enter into no correspondence upon
this matter.

Osprey Publishing supports the Woodland Trust, the UK's leading woodland
conservation charity.

To find out more about our authors and books, visit
www.ospreypublishing.com. Here you will find extracts, author
interviews, details of forthcoming events and the option to sign up for
our newsletter.

Author's acknowledgements

I wish to thank Mr Nik Cornish of Stavka.org, and the staff of the
Bundesarchiv and Süddeutsche Zeitung (SDZ) for their help with
this project.

Author's dedication

In remembrance of 1LT Weston Lee, platoon leader in 1-325 Airborne
Infantry Regiment, KIA, Mosul, Iraq on 29 April 2017.

Key to military symbols

CONTENTS

The strategic situation on the Eastern Front, 6 August 1943

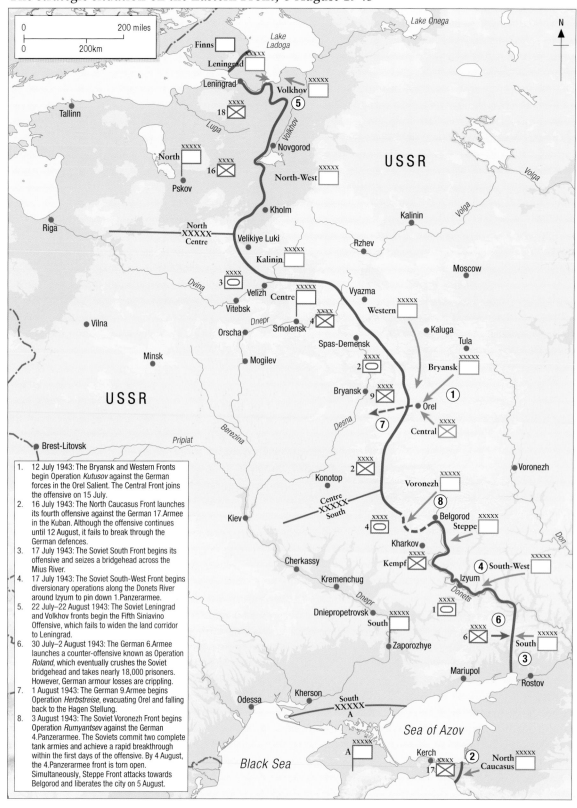

0 ____ 200 miles
0 ____ 200km

N

Lake Onega

Finns ☐
XXXX

Lake Ladoga

Leningrad
Leningrad
Volkhov ☐
XXXXX
⑤

18 ☒
XXXX

Tallinn

Luga

North ☐
XXXXX
Pskov

16 ☒
XXXX

Novgorod

North-West ☐
XXXXX

USSR

Kholm

Kalinin

Volga

Riga

North
XXXXX
Centre

Velikiye Luki

Rzhev

Moscow

Kalinin ☐
XXXXX

Dvina

3 ⬭
XXXX

Velizh
Centre ☐
XXXXX

Vyazma

Vitebsk

Vilna

Dnepr
Orscha

Smolensk

4 ☒
XXXX

Western ☐
XXXXX

Kaluga

Tula

Minsk

Mogilev

Spas-Demensk

2 ⬭
XXXX

Bryansk ☐
XXXXX

USSR

Bryansk

9 ☒
XXXX

Orel

①

Central ☒
XXXX

Desna

⑦

Brest-Litovsk

Pripiat

Berezina

Voronezh

1. 12 July 1943: The Bryansk and Western Fronts begin Operation *Kutusov* against the German forces in the Orel Salient. The Central Front joins the offensive on 15 July.
2. 16 July 1943: The North Caucasus Front launches its fourth offensive against the German 17.Armee in the Kuban. Although the offensive continues until 12 August, it fails to break through the German defences.
3. 17 July 1943: The Soviet South Front begins its offensive and seizes a bridgehead across the Mius River.
4. 17 July 1943: The Soviet South-West Front begins diversionary operations along the Donets River around Izyum to pin down 1.Panzerarmee.
5. 22 July–22 August 1943: The Soviet Leningrad and Volkhov fronts begin the Fifth Siniavino Offensive, which fails to widen the land corridor to Leningrad.
6. 30 July–2 August 1943: The German 6.Armee launches a counter-offensive known as Operation *Roland*, which eventually crushes the Soviet bridgehead and takes nearly 18,000 prisoners. However, German armour losses are crippling.
7. 1 August 1943: The German 9.Armee begins Operation *Herbstreise*, evacuating Orel and falling back to the Hagen Stellung.
8. 3 August 1943: The Soviet Voronezh Front begins Operation *Rumyantsev* against the German 4.Panzerarmee. The Soviets commit two complete tank armies and achieve a rapid breakthrough within the first days of the offensive. By 4 August, the 4.Panzerarmee front is torn open. Simultaneously, Steppe Front attacks towards Belgorod and liberates the city on 5 August.

Konotop

2 ☒
XXXX

Voronezh ☐
XXXXX

⑧

Centre
XXXXX
South

4 ⬭
XXXX

Belgorod
Steppe ☐
XXXXX

Kharkov

Kiev

Kempf ☒
XXXX

South-West ☐
XXXXX
④

Izyum

Don

Cherkassy

Kremenchug

1 ⬭
XXXX

Donets

⑥

Dnepr

Dniepropetrovsk

South ☐
XXXXX

6 ☒
XXXX

South ☐
XXXXX

③

Zaporozhye

Mariupol

Rostov

Odessa

Kherson

South
XXXXX
A

Sea of Azov

A ☐
XXXXX

Kerch

17 ☒
XXXX

②

North Caucasus ☐
XXXXX

Black Sea

ORIGINS OF THE CAMPAIGN

When the German Wehrmacht invaded the Soviet Union in June 1941, it expected to make short work of the Soviet Red Army. In the opening weeks of the campaign, the Soviet Western Front (Zapadnyy Front) was badly defeated by the German Heeresgruppe Mitte (Army Group Centre) in the Battle of Bialystok-Minsk, then smashed again in the Battle of Smolensk in July 1941. After Smolensk was lost, the Western Front managed to regroup and establish a new line to defend the approaches to Moscow. Hitler and the German High Command (Oberkommando des Heeres, or OKH) were astonished by Soviet resilience but resolved to make one last all-out effort to achieve a decisive victory before the arrival of winter weather. In late September 1941, Heeresgruppe Mitte launched Operation *Typhoon* with Moscow as its ultimate objective. Once again, German Panzer spearheads quickly sliced through the Soviet linear defences and surrounded the bulk of the rebuilt Western Front in the Vyazma-Bryansk pockets before the Soviet High Command (Stavka) could react. In desperation, Stalin assigned General Georgy Zhukov to reorganize the battered remnants of the Western Front and ordered him to make a last-ditch stand outside Moscow. Zhukov's tenacious defence, combined with German supply problems and increasingly adverse weather conditions, halted Operation *Typhoon* just short of its goal. Although overextended, Heeresgruppe Mitte might have been able to hold most of the territory conquered up to this point, had not Zhukov launched a brilliant winter counter-offensive before the Germans could establish proper defensive positions. Amidst bitter freezing cold temperatures and deep snow, Heeresgruppe Mitte was forced to retreat from Moscow, abandoning a good deal of its artillery and vehicles in the process.

However, Zhukov's impromptu counter-offensive lacked the resources to finish off the retreating Heeresgruppe Mitte and Hitler ordered German units to establish *Stützpunkte* (strongpoints) in fortified towns, which helped to slow the Red Army's advance. By early January 1942, Zhukov's counter-offensive was running out of steam, but the front remained fluid until the spring. Heeresgruppe Mitte's 9.Armee was left holding the vulnerable Rzhev salient – which Hitler refused to abandon – as well as Vyazma and Bryansk. Some Soviet units managed to fight their way to within 30km of Smolensk and a cavalry corps briefly occupied the Minsk–Moscow Highway west of Smolensk, but these forces could not be supplied and were soon isolated. In a bold bid to unhinge the German defence of Vyazma, Zhukov decided to drop four airborne brigades with 11,000 paratroopers around that city, but Soviet ground forces failed to link up with the air-landed troops. In

The Germans captured Smolensk on 16 July 1941 after a tough defensive fight by the Western Front. Although damaged, the city was still habitable and it would soon become a key logistic hub for Heeresgruppe Mitte in 1942–43. (Süddeutsche Zeitung Bild 00399849, Foto: Scherl)

February 1942, Heeresgruppe Mitte had regained just enough strength to begin launching local counterattacks. Generaloberst Gotthard Heinrici's 4.Armee managed to isolate the Western Front's 33rd Army south-east of Vyazma, while Generaloberst Walter Model's 9.Armee cut off the 39th Army from the Karelian Front north of Vyazma. Although it would take months for the Germans to mop up these pockets, both trapped Soviet armies were eventually annihilated. Nevertheless, many of the isolated paratroopers and soldiers joined up with local partisans and remained a serious threat to Heeresgruppe Mitte's lines of communications for some time. While Heinrici's 4.Armee managed to establish a fairly solid defence along most of its front by June 1942, the greatest threat to Heeresgruppe Mitte remained the thinly held 3.Panzerarmee sector between Velikiye Luki and Vyazma. General-polkovnik Ivan S. Konev's Kalinin Front had driven a deep wedge between 3.Panzerarmee and 9.Armee, and elements of its 4th Shock Army were just 50km north of Smolensk.

As spring blossomed, the main focus of the war in the east shifted to the southern theatre, around Kharkov and the Crimea. While most Eastern Front histories tend to ignore the central combat zone during much of 1942–43, Heeresgruppe Mitte remained locked in a constant battle of attrition with the Kalinin and Western fronts. Zhukov was determined to destroy Heeresgruppe Mitte and ensured that his Western Front – not the Red Army forces in the south – had priority for reinforcements in mid-1942. Stalin, who was concerned about a new German offensive towards Moscow, supported this policy. Although the Kalinin Front was better situated to inflict damage upon the overextended left flank of Heeresgruppe Mitte, Zhukov was unwilling to

share laurels with his rival Konev and decided that the main effort in 1942 would be made by his forces against the centre and right of the German front.

On 5 July 1942, Zhukov's Western Front began a major offensive against 2.Panzerarmee in the Zhizdra-Bolkhov sector with the 16th and 61st armies. Despite the commitment of two tank corps, German infantry divisions in this sector held firm and inflicted great losses upon the attacking Soviets. Von Kluge committed two *Panzer-Divisionen* and extensive Luftwaffe support to the Zhizdra-Bolkhov sector, which halted Zhukov's offensive. Indeed, Soviet forces were in such disarray that von Kluge decided to mass five *Panzer-Divisionen* to mount a local counter-offensive known as Operation *Wirbelwind*, which managed to push the Soviets back to their start line. Undeterred, Zhukov decided to pause the offensive against 2.Panzerarmee and instead began an even larger offensive against the Rzhev salient. He assigned Konev's Kalinin Front a supporting role in the Rzhev operation, but provided it with only minimal air, artillery and armour support. Konev attacked the west side of the Rzhev salient on 30 July 1942 with the 29th and 30th armies, but made no progress. Once 9.Armee was focused on Konev's attacks, Zhukov attacked the eastern side of the salient four days later with the 20th and 31st armies. By massing 600 tanks on a narrow sector and providing effective air support, Zhukov was able to achieve a breakthrough – this was the first time that the Red Army succeeded in breaching a German solid defensive line – but he was slow to exploit his success. Von Kluge promptly provided 9.Armee with two *Panzer-Divisionen*, which were used to delay the Soviet advance. After three weeks of costly fighting, Zhukov's advance was finally halted, without cutting off the Rzhev salient or destroying

German soldiers from 260. Infanterie-Division man a section of trench in the Büffel-Stellung in 1943. Ample timber helped to reinforce trenches but also tended to substantially reduce fields of fire. Although 4.Armee held a relatively quiet sector of the Eastern Front in the summer of 1943, the daily casualties from snipers, artillery and patrol action quickly reduced infantry units to about half their authorized establishment. By August 1943, the Wehrmacht was no longer receiving the quality or quantity of replacements to preserve its edge in defensive combat over the Red Army. (Author's collection)

German troops constructing new defensive positions, spring 1943. After the retreat from the Rzhev salient, 4.Armee built a series of fortified lines to protect its new, shortened front. Once positions like this were completed, they were relatively immune to Soviet light artillery fire. The absence of obvious firing positions suggests that this bunker is probably located in a second line of defence, possibly for a battalion-level aid station or supply point. (From Nik Cornish@ Stavka.org.uk)

9.Armee. Unwilling to admit failure, Zhukov decided to resume his effort against 2.Panzerarmee and committed his trump card – the 700 tanks of the 3rd Tank Army – on 22 August. Attacking into the teeth of an alert German defence backed by several *Panzer-Divisionen* was a major mistake and the Soviet tank army was shot to pieces in days, losing 70 per cent of its armour. The Soviet summer offensive against Heeresgruppe Mitte was a failure and German forces were still within 240km of Moscow.

Despite the main German effort occurring in the south, with Heeresgruppe B advancing towards the Volga and Heeresgruppe A pushing into the Caucasus, Zhukov remained committed to destroying Heeresgruppe Mitte. He succeeded in convincing Stalin that his attack on the Rzhev salient was a near success, and in late September he was authorized to conduct another major joint offensive by the Kalinin and Western fronts against 9.Armee. Once again, Zhukov persuaded Stalin to provide the Western Front with massive reinforcements of men and materiel. Zhukov planned Operation *Mars* as another pincer attack, with the Kalinin Front (now under General-polkovnik Maksim A. Purkaev) assaulting the west side of the salient with the 22nd, 39th and 41st armies, while Zhukov's Western Front attacked the east side with the 20th Army. Altogether, Operation *Mars* concentrated over 800,000 Soviet troops and 2,000 tanks against the German 9.Armee. Zhukov's grand offensive began on 25 November 1942 and achieved local breakthroughs in three locations. Although stressed to the breaking point, Model fought a series of brilliant delaying actions until von Kluge was able to transfer three *Panzer-Divisionen* to 9.Armee. After initial success, the

Soviet attacks bogged down and Model began launching counterattacks in early December, which cut off the Soviet spearhead units. In three weeks of heavy combat, 9.Armee annihilated six elite Soviet corps, which forced Zhukov to call off Operation *Mars* on 20 December 1942. It had been a costly year for both sides. During 1942, Heeresgruppe Mitte suffered over 357,000 casualties while the Kalinin and Western fronts suffered a combined total of 1.8 million casualties.

While Heeresgruppe Mitte had succeeded in defeating three major Soviet offensives in 1942, it was clear after the debacle at Stalingrad that the Wehrmacht could not indefinitely sustain this level of attrition. Even Model recognized that holding the Rzhev salient was no longer worth the cost and he managed to persuade Hitler to authorize its evacuation. Furthermore, the *Panzer-Divisionen* used to stop Zhukov's offensives were desperately needed to restore the broken front in the south. Consequently, in March 1943 Heeresgruppe Mitte conducted Operation *Büffel* (*Buffalo*), evacuating the Rzhev salient. As a result of *Büffel*, Heeresgruppe Mitte's frontage was reduced from a length of 754km to just 386km. Before the evacuation began, German *Pionier* troops constructed a new defensive line that was consciously modelled on the 1917 Siegfried-Stellung. By late March 1943, the Germans had occupied the new positions and von Kluge's front was significantly shorter and less vulnerable.

Both von Kluge and Model advocated using the newly released divisions to create a mobile reserve, but instead Hitler directed that 9.Armee would be transferred to the Orel salient in order to participate in his next summer offensive, designated Operation *Zitadelle*. All of Heeresgruppe Mitte's *Panzer-Divisionen* were allocated to Model's 9.Armee for *Zitadelle*, leaving von Kluge with hardly any mobile reserves. After Rzhev was abandoned, Heeresgruppe Mitte settled into static – but costly – positional warfare, which cost it another 137,000 casualties in the first six months of 1943. Both the Kalinin and Western fronts mounted local probing attacks in up to battalion strength on a nearly daily basis, but the only Soviet success during this period was the destruction of the German garrison in Velikiye Luki. Heinrici's 4.Armee, now holding the centre of Heeresgruppe Mitte's sector, used the time to improve its defences in depth and to fortify all the front-line towns in its area. While Heeresgruppe Mitte had been steadily stripped of resources in order to feed the advance to the Volga in 1942 and then Operation *Zitadelle* in 1943, it still possessed the resources to mount a determined defence of the Smolensk-Bryansk sectors.

From the Soviet perspective, the liberation of Rzhev in March 1943 was a hollow accomplishment in itself, but it set the stage for a new Soviet grand offensive to retake the important cities of Vyazma, Bryansk and Smolensk. A frustrated Zhukov went to Leningrad to direct a renewed effort to open a land corridor to the encircled city – which succeeded – and then Stavka (the Soviet High Command) shifted its attention back to the Kharkov region. Once the Soviet winter counter-offensives ceased, both the OKH and Stavka paused to consider their next moves. In particular, Stavka was aware that the Germans were planning one last major offensive against the Kursk salient, Operation *Zitadelle*. Once this offensive was defeated and the German reserves expended, Stavka intended to unleash a series of coordinated front-level offensives that would permanently break the Wehrmacht's combat power in the East.

CHRONOLOGY

1943

3 August   Soviet partisans begin Operation *Rail War* against Heeresgruppe Mitte's rail lines.

7 August   Operation *Suvorov* begins, but Soviet forces make only limited gains.

12 August   Hitler authorizes the Ostwall (East Wall – later called the 'Panther-Stellung').

13 August   Sokolovsky commits the 5th Mechanized Corps to battle. Spas-Demensk is liberated.

               The Kalinin Front joins the offensive.

21 August   The *Suvorov* operation is temporarily suspended in order to resupply combat units.

23 August   The Kalinin Front resumes its offensive.

28 August   *Suvorov* recommences. The 2nd Guards Tank Corps advances 30km in a single day.

30 August   Yelnya is liberated.

1 September   Dorogobuzh is liberated.

7 September   After reaching the Dnepr, Sokolovsky pauses the offensive again.

8 September   Construction finally begins on the Panther-Stellung.

14 September The Kalinin Front attacks.

16 September The Western Front attacks and captures Yartsevo.

17 September The 39th Army liberates Dukhovshchina.

19 September 4.Armee begins to retreat to the Panther-Stellung after its front is broken.

               Soviet partisans initiate Operation *Kontsert* (*Concert*) against Heeresgruppe Mitte rail lines.

25 September The Soviet 5th Army liberates Smolensk and Roslavl.

29 September The 4.Armee begins to occupy the Panther-Stellung.

OPPOSING COMMANDERS

SOVIET

Like all Soviet front-level commands, decision-making in the Western Front resided in the military council, with the military represented by the front commander and his chief of staff, General-leytenant Aleksandr P. Pokrovsky. However, Stalin's interests were represented by Nikolai A. Bulganin, who had a dominant voice on the council. In addition, another party figure, Ivan S. Khokhlov, served as chief of the Western Front's Political Section. Bulganin and Khokhlov were both politicians, not soldiers, but their views played a major role in the Western Front's decision-making. A strong military leader like Zhukov could still steer a party-dominated military council to endorse his decisions, but Sokolovsky lacked that flair.

General Vasily D. Sokolovsky (1897–1968) had been commander of the Western Front since February 1943. Sokolovsky had been a staff officer for most of his career in the Red Army and he was a protégé of Georgy Zhukov, but lacked his self-assurance. As the chief of staff for the Western Front in 1942, Sokolovsky presided over the failed Zhizdra-Bolkhov offensive in July–August 1942 as well as Operation *Mars* in November 1942 – not exactly a stellar record of success. Stavka regarded Sokolovsky as cautious. Indeed, he was more of a resource manager and high-level paper-pusher than a battlefield commander. Yet by mid-1943, the Red Army still only had a handful of really effective front-level commanders and had to make do with a number of mediocre officers like Sokolovsky, who were at least capable of following orders.

General Vasily D. Sokolovsky, commander of the Western Front. Sokolovsky was a deliberate, careful commander who could plan an operation. However, he lacked the ruthless energy of Zhukov and Konev. (Author's collection)

General-polkovnik Andrei I. Eremenko (1892–1970) was promoted commander of the Kalinin Front in April 1943. Eremenko was a Ukrainian cavalryman who first saw action with the Tsarist Army in World War I, then the Red Army. Thanks to a certain cavalry-style panache, Eremenko rose rapidly during the interwar period, but was still junior enough to survive the Stalinist

General-polkovnik Andrei I. Eremenko, commander of the Kalinin Front. Eremenko had not fully recovered from serious wounds received during the fighting in 1941, and both his physical health and mental attitude were sub-par in August 1943. (Author's collection)

Marshal of Artillery Nikolai N. Voronov, Stavka representative to the Western Front. Voronov played a major role in the artillery support planning for Operation *Suvorov* but his efforts were hampered by persistent ammunition shortages. While very political, Voronov was an expert in front-level planning and coordination. (Author's collection)

purges. In July 1941, he took over the retreating Western Front and was ordered to stop the Germans at Smolensk, but was wounded after only ten days in command. After a brief recovery, Eremenko was assigned to command the Bryansk Front, which was hard hit by Operation *Typhoon*, and he was wounded again. During the Moscow winter counter-offensive, Eremenko successfully led the 4th Shock Army, but afterwards he was side-lined by his injuries for six months. Although not fully recovered, Eremenko was sent in August 1942 to command the South-East Front, which soon became the Stalingrad Front. He played a major role in the defence of that city, as well as the counter-offensive that surrounded the German 6.Armee. However, Eremenko was dragged into political squabbling between Stalin and Nikita Khrushchev (the front commissar) and he criticized some of Stalin's military decisions, which hurt his standing with the Soviet leader. For his part, Eremenko was annoyed that Stalin failed to congratulate him for his role in the victory at Stalingrad and regarded his assignment to the Kalinin Front as something of a demotion. At his best, Eremenko was a competent, aggressive commander who also displayed a very hands-on style with the troops.

Marshal of Artillery Nikolai N. Voronov (1899–1968) had been Stavka representative to the Western Front since August 1943. Voronov joined the Red Army in 1918 and served as an artilleryman in the Polish-Soviet War, in which he was captured. Afterwards, he distinguished himself in the interwar period and served briefly as an advisor in Spain in 1937. Voronov benefitted from the purges, which resulted in his being catapulted to the head of the Red Army's artillery branch. Voronov had a lucky career: he led Soviet artillery units at the Battle of Khalkhin Gol in 1939, then planned the artillery offensive that smashed the Finnish Mannerheim Line in 1940. By 1941, Voronov was made a Deputy People's Commissar for Defence and served as a Stavka representative in the defence of Leningrad. He served in the same capacity at Stalingrad in 1942, orchestrating Soviet artillery to crush the final resistance of the trapped German 6.Armee. Voronov also participated in the interrogation of the 6.Armee commander, Generalfeldmarschall Friedrich Paulus, which no doubt gave him some insight into German operational methods. In early 1943, Voronov was instrumental in re-organizing Soviet artillery into larger corps-size units and helping to plan the defence of the Kursk salient. Voronov was a skilled artillery planner and experienced at coordinating multi-front operations.

General-leytenant Mikhail M. Gromov (1899–1985) was appointed commander of the 1st Air Army in May 1943. Gromov had originally trained as a pilot in 1918 and was something of an intellectual, which enabled him to serve in research roles in the Flight Research Institute for most of the interwar period. He was a talented test pilot and an aviation pioneer, establishing a long-distance flight record in 1937. However, Gromov had negligible command or combat experience at the start of World War II. Nevertheless, he was made commander of an aviation division on the Kalinin Front in 1941–42 and then given command of one of the first air armies, 3rd Air Army, in 1942–43. Gromov was mis-cast as a senior aviation commander and would have been better utilized in developing new combat aircraft for the Soviet Air Force (*Voyenno-Vozdushnye Sily*, VVS), but the exigencies of wartime required him to serve as a front-line commander.

General-leytenant Kuzma P. Trubnikov (1888–1974) was appointed commander of the 10th Guards Army in May 1943. Trubnikov had served as an NCO in the Imperial Guard in the Tsarist Army and was highly decorated for bravery in combat during World War I. He joined the Red Army in 1918 as a 'military specialist' and rose rapidly from platoon leader to infantry brigade commander in the Russian Civil War. Afterwards, Trubnikov graduated from the Frunze Military Academy, but was arrested and spent two years in prison during the Stalinist purges. He was reinstated in 1941 and played a prominent role in defending Tula against Generaloberst Heinz Guderian's panzers. In 1942, Trubnikov served as deputy commander of the Don Front during the Battle of Stalingrad. Trubnikov was a solid military professional, well versed in handling large formations in combat. However, he was blamed for the initial failures in *Suvorov* and removed from command of the 10th Guards Army after the liberation of Yelnya. He held no further major commands for the duration of the war.

General-leytenant Mikhail M. Gromov, commander of the 1st Air Army. Although renowned as a Soviet aviation pioneer, Gromov lacked the background to be an effective commander of a large-scale aviation formation and his units performed well below par in the opening phase of the offensive. (Author's collection)

GERMAN

Even with interference from Hitler, German decision-making in Heeresgruppe Mitte was far more streamlined and professional than in the Western Front's committee process. All the principle German military leaders were highly trained and experienced officers, although politically they included members who secretly opposed Hitler's regime and those who fanatically sought to defend Germany and the Third Reich at all costs.

Generalfeldmarschall Günther von Kluge (1882–1944) was appointed commander of Heeresgruppe Mitte in December 1941. Von Kluge came from a Prussian military family and was commissioned as an artillery officer in 1901. During World War I, he served as a General Staff officer on the Western Front and was later retained in the post-war Reichswehr. Von Kluge was astute at political manoeuvring to gain favour with the Nazis, even though he despised them. At the start of World War II, von Kluge was given command of 4.Armee, which he successfully led in the Polish and French campaigns, as well as Operation *Barbarossa*. Von Kluge was a competent commander, but he was averse to taking serious risks and did not always work well with others. During the Moscow campaign in 1941, von Kluge conducted dilatory operations in order to reduce the risk to his own command, which contributed to the German failure. Despite a lacklustre performance in Operation *Typhoon*, von Kluge was rewarded with command of Heeresguppe Mitte after Generalfeldmarschall Fedor von Bock was relieved of command. As army group commander, von Kluge granted considerable autonomy to his subordinate commanders such as Walter Model and Gotthard Heinrici, preferring to focus on 'the big picture'. In October 1943, von Kluge was severely injured in a car accident and was transferred to the Führer Reserve for the next eight months.

Generaloberst Gotthard Heinrici (1886–1971) had been commander of 4.Armee since January 1942. Heinrici was another typical East Prussian officer and was a cousin of Gerd von Rundstedt. During World War I, he fought as a junior infantry officer on both the Western and Eastern fronts, before being trained as a General Staff officer. After the war, Heinrici was retained in the Reichswehr and dabbled in right-wing politics, but did not join the Nazis. He served as a corps commander during the French campaign in 1940 and during Operation *Barbarossa* in 1941. As an army commander, Heinrici gained a reputation during the winter of 1941/42 as a superb defensive tactician; his most successful tactic was to determine where a Soviet offensive was likely and then temporarily thin out the front line in that sector in order to avoid the enemy's artillery preparation – then reoccupy the positions. Heinrici was a religious man, which led to friction with Nazi Party officials who tried to sabotage his career, but he was protected by von Kluge, who needed him to hold the crucial Smolensk sector.

Generaloberst Robert Ritter von Greim (1892–1945) was appointed commander of Luftflotte 6 in May 1943. Von Greim joined the Bavarian Army in 1911 and served in the opening stages of World War I as a junior artillery officer. In the summer of 1915, he transferred to the aviation service and served as an observer before receiving pilot training in 1916. Von Greim had a very successful career as a fighter pilot in 1917–18, achieving 28 victories, which gained him the award of the Pour le Mérite. After the war, he became an early follower of Hitler, joining the Nazi Party and participating in the failed 1923 Putsch. In return for his loyalty, von Greim played a critical role in the creation of the Luftwaffe between 1933 and 1937. At the start of World War II, he commanded 5.Flieger-Division in the Polish Campaign. Afterwards, his command became V Fliegerkorps, which von Greim led between 1940 and 1942. By 1943, von Greim was an experienced front-line aviation commander and still thoroughly committed to defending the Third Reich.

OPPOSING FORCES

SOVIET

Altogether, the Western Front had 824,000 troops and 61 divisions. Sokolovsky intended to use 16 divisions in the first echelon of Operation *Suvorov*, then 22 more divisions in the second echelon of the offensive. The remaining forces, of lower combat capability, were assigned only defensive missions. Eremenko's Kalinin Front had 428,000 troops in 26 divisions. The Soviet forces arrayed for Operation *Suvorov* were powerful and numerous, but suffered from serious logistic shortfalls. In particular, Eremenko's troops were plagued by persistent food shortages that left many of his front-line troops malnourished.

Infantry

By early 1943, heavy personnel losses had forced the Red Army to reduce the manning structure of its rifle divisions, to just 9,300 troops each, but even this new level proved unsustainable at the front. At the start of Operation *Suvorov*, rifle divisions in the Western Front's 5th, 31st and 33rd armies averaged about 6,500–7,000 troops each (about 70–75 per cent of their authorized strength), whereas the Guards Rifle divisions in the 10th Guards Army were slightly stronger, with about 8,000 troops each. A 20,000–25,000-man rifle corps, comprised of three rifle divisions, became the basis of each army's shock groups. In order to make up for fewer troops, the rifle divisions were provided with more sub-machine guns, but otherwise had the same amount of support weapons as the previous divisions. Sokolovsky intended to use 25 of his rifle divisions to form the main shock groups, while the rest either conducted supporting attacks or held quiet sectors on the flanks.

In October 1942, Soviet infantry doctrine was revised and required divisions to attack in a single echelon on a 4–5km-wide front, in order to maximize combat power in the initial stage of an attack. For *Suvorov*, the Western Front reduced the attack frontage for each rifle division to just 2–2.5km. Each rifle corps would attack with two divisions up front, while their third division was used as a second echelon formation. By mid-1943, the Red Army had refined its tactics, in an effort to employ more pre-battle reconnaissance and engineers to clear obstacles. Instead of just relying upon masses of infantry as in the 1941–42 offensives, the Red Army of 1943 recognized that it needed to adopt combined-arms tactics in order to breach German defences in depth – but it was still experiencing difficulty in actually using them.

Armour/cavalry

Since all of Sokolovsky's tank corps were already committed to Operation *Kutusov* in the Orel salient, the only large mechanized formation left available for Operation *Suvorov* was General-leytenant Mikhail V. Volkhov's 5th Mechanized Corps. The 5th Mechanized Corps had been in the *Rezerv Verkhovnogo Glavnokomandovaniya* (RVGK – Stavka Reserve) for the past four months and was at full strength, with 193 tanks and 20 assault guns. All of the 5th Mechanized Corps' tanks were British-made Matildas and Valentines, which the Soviets regarded as second-rate in terms of mobility and firepower to their own T-34 tank. To support the breakthrough battle, the Western Front allocated four independent tank brigades and three tank regiments to the assault groups, a total of about 300 tanks. Most of these tank units were committed to the infantry support role, but a few of the veteran units, such as the 42nd Guards Tank Brigade, were used to form army-level mobile groups. The Red Army leadership was introducing new methods for employing its armour and recognized the importance of achieving a clean breakthrough with infantry-artillery-close support tanks before trying to commit a mechanized mobile group to strike deeper targets.

Altogether, the Western Front had 961 tanks and about 40 assault guns, while the Kalinin Front could add another 110 tanks, giving the Red Army a decisive numerical advantage over the German 4.Armee. Furthermore, the T-34/76 medium tank was superior to the small number of German PzKpfw III and IV medium tanks in this sector. Since Soviet production was still struggling to churn out enough T-34s to meet demands, Soviet tank brigades in August 1943 still had a significant number of T-60/70 light tanks and even a few KV-1 heavy tanks. In the weeks just prior to the offensive, Sokolovsky received 300 new tanks, in order to bring his front-line tank units up to strength. Unfortunately, Sokolovsky did not receive adequate fuel to support major mechanized operations due to the needs of other fronts.

The Western and Kalinin fronts also intended to use mixed tank-cavalry groups in the exploitation role, as well. Given the wooded nature of the terrain and fuel shortage, this was a sensible decision. The Western Front had General-mayor Sergei V. Sokolov's 6th Guards Cavalry Corps, which was a mixed group with over 5,000 mounted troops, supported by 110 tanks and 20 Su-76 assault guns. The Kalinin Front had General-mayor Nikolai S. Oslikovsky's 3rd Guards Cavalry Corps, which was similar in composition. By this point in the war, the Red Army was finding it difficult to replace its horse losses and the mounted component of cavalry units was continually reduced.

Artillery

Stavka provided the Western Front with General-mayor Mikhail P. Kuteinikov's 5th Breakthrough Artillery Corps to spearhead Operation *Suvorov*. General-Polkovnik Ivan P. Kamera, artillery commander of the Western Front, assigned the 3rd Guards Artillery Division to support the 5th Army and the 4th Guards Artillery Division to the 33rd Army, but kept the 7th Guards Mortar Division under front control. The 4th Guards Artillery Division was specially tasked with using its 152mm howitzers in the counter-battery role to suppress German artillery positions; it formed a Long-Range Artillery Group (*Artillerii Dal'nego Deystviya* – ADD) for this purpose. Along with other independent army-level artillery units, the Western Front deployed 3,445 artillery pieces, 5,131 mortars and about 500 rocket-

The Soviet trump card in Operation *Suvorov* was intended to be the artillery, particularly the long-range guns of the 5th Breakthrough Artillery Corps. Here, a 152mm ML-20 howitzer prepares to fire. (Courtesy of the Central Museum of the Armed Forces, Moscow via www. Stavka.org.uk)

A group of La-5FN fighters from 2nd Soviet Guards Fighter Aviation Regiment (GIAP). The pilot in the foreground is Leytenant Aleksandr I. Mayorov, who was already an ace by August 1943. The La-5FN was a solid fighter that could match the German Fw-190, when it had an experienced pilot in the cockpit. However, the VVS in mid-1943 still had far too many novice pilots. (Author's collection)

launchers to support Operation *Suvorov*. Altogether, in the main attack sectors, Kamera massed about 165 tubes (76.2mm or larger) per kilometre. A significant proportion of the Soviet artillery consisted of multiple rocket-launchers, including over 200 of the new M-31 launchers in the 7th Guards Mortar Division and about 300 launchers in separate units.

Sokolovsky and Voronov intended to use massed artillery fire to reduce enemy strongpoints and then push on into the depth of the enemy's positions. The Red Army had developed the ability to mass a large volume of artillery fire, but fire-support planning was hindered by inadequate information on enemy positions beyond the immediate front line. Too often, Soviet artillery fire blasted lightly held forward positions in the enemy's security zone but barely touched the German *Hauptkampflinie* (HKL – Main Line of Resistance) or artillery positions. Furthermore, Soviet artillery support during *Suvorov* was undermined by the inadequate amount of ammunition stockpiled for the operation. The Western Front artillery received only 2.5 units of fire per battery, which was reckoned just enough to last for four days. The Kalinin Front received much less ammunition.

Aviation

Gromov's 1st Air Army could commit over 1,000 operational combat aircraft to Operation *Suvorov*, ensuring an overall numerical superiority of 3:1 on paper over Luftflotte 6. Papivin's 3rd Air Army could add another 200 aircraft to support the operation. Altogether, 1st Air Army and 3rd Air Army were expected to fly about 2,500 operational sorties on the first day of the offensive, hopefully gaining air superiority over the critical sectors. However, Soviet aviation units had lower serviceability and sortie rates than their German opponents, along with persistent fuel shortages, which evened up the odds a bit. Whereas most Soviet fighter regiments averaged 0.5 sorties per aircraft/day, Luftwaffe fighters often flew two to three sorties per day; this meant the theoretical Soviet 4.5:1 edge in fighters in this sector was reduced to about 1:1 in reality. Furthermore, the most prevalent fighter model in 1st Air Army was the Yak-7B, which was outclassed in terms of speed and firepower by Jagdgeschwader (JG) 51's Fw-190A-5 fighters. Soviet industry was succeeding in producing large numbers of combat aircraft, but quality control was poor and many aircraft delivered to the front suffered from defects. In terms of pilots, the VVS fighter units had far fewer veterans than their opponents and the tactics of their hastily trained pilots were often rudimentary. In August 1943, two-thirds of VVS pilots were fresh from training units, where they typically received only 20–30 hours of flight time, against 200–250 hours for new Luftwaffe pilots.

The VVS was still plagued by operational shortcomings, as well. For example, the air armies still had difficulty coordinating their various units in order to achieve maximum combat synergy, such as ensuring that fighters arrived in time to escort bombers and ground-attack aircraft. Mission-planning and target selection also remained problematic. Instead of using the 100 operational Pe-2 bombers in the 2nd *Bombardirovochnaya Aviatsionnyi Korpus* (BAK – Bomber Aviation Corps) to make massed strikes against a single priority target, the 1st Air Army employed them as individual regiments against diverse targets. The most potent force available to 1st Air Army was the 2nd *Shturmovoy Aviatsionnyi Korpus* (ShAK – Ground Attack Aviation Corps), which could employ almost 200 Il-2 Sturmoviks in the ground support role; when massed, low-level Sturmovik attacks could be devastating. However, the VVS tended to assign some Sturmoviks to support each assaulting army, thereby reducing 2nd ShAK's overall contribution to the campaign. By late 1943, Soviet airpower was growing in effectiveness, but was still challenged to accomplish its missions when up against the best Luftwaffe units.

Partisans

Significant numbers of Soviet troops had been left behind in the Smolensk region in 1941–42 and many eventually became partisans. According to Soviet sources, there were roughly 60,000 partisans in the Smolensk region, but this was likely exaggerated. According to a very detailed report from the German 286.Sicherungs-Division, based in Orscha, in July 1943 there were 20 Soviet brigade-size partisan units operating in the Heeresgruppe Mitte sector, with a combined total of 17,000–21,000 armed personnel. The German report included considerable detail on unit commanders, operating areas and equipment, presumably acquired through prisoner interrogations. The partisan brigades were built upon smaller sub-units known as *Otryadi*, which typically consisted of 100–150 personnel each. Most partisan brigades in mid-1943 had 500–1,000 personnel, but one unit – Brigade Melnikov operating west of Vitebsk – was believed to have 3,500–5,000 personnel. Most units were equipped with small arms, light machine guns and mortars, but several units had light artillery or anti-tank guns.

During 1941–42, the partisans conducted independent and localized harassing operations in the German rear areas, but failed to achieve any significant successes. After a year of the partisans being on their own, in mid-1942 Stavka finally decided to take control over their disparate units and began dropping radios, weapons and explosives to them by parachute. By mid-1943, Stavka had embedded trusted regional commanders with the partisans to coordinate the actions of various partisan units, thereby creating enough synergy to provide tangible support to Red Army offensive operations. In early August 1943, Stavka ordered partisan units in the Smolensk and Bryansk regions to step up attacks against Heeresgruppe Mitte's rail lines, just prior to the beginning of *Suvorov*; this campaign was designated Operation *Rel'sovaya Voyna* (*Rail War*).

GERMAN

The primary German formation opposing Operation *Suvorov* was Heinrici's 4.Armee, consisting of about 250,000 troops in six subordinate corps, which controlled a total of 18 divisions at the start of the campaign. Rear-area forces were commanded by Korück 559, which was essentially a corps-size security force. The Luftwaffe provided air support with Luftflotte 6 and ground support with 18.Flak-Division. Overall, the German forces defending the Smolensk–Roslavl region were well-led veteran troops, but undermined by material shortages and lack of reserves.

Infantry

By August 1943, the German *Ostheer* (Army in the East) was unable to replace its personnel losses and many infantry divisions could no longer maintain a nine-battalion organizational structure. Instead, many of 4.Armee's divisions were already reduced to a two infantry regiment structure (with a total of six infantry battalions) and were forced to fill gaps with their *Pioniere* and Feldersatz-Bataillon (Field Replacement Battalion). Another improvisation was the creation of a 'Division Battalion', which incorporated various elements from disbanded units. The only infantry division near full strength was 113.Infanterie-Division in XXXIX Panzerkorps, but it was a newly raised unit intended to replace the original division lost six months before at Stalingrad. About 80 per cent of 113.Infanterie-Division's troops consisted of personnel transferred from the Luftwaffe or new recruits; after four months training in France, the division was transferred to the Russian front just two weeks before *Suvorov* commenced. Furthermore, the divisional commander – Generalmajor Friedrich-Wilhelm Prüter – had experienced combat as a junior

A German MG34 machine-gun crew scan the horizon, looking for signs of the enemy. German defensive tactics were heavily based on the integration of automatic weapons, mortars and artillery support to prevent the numerically superior Soviets from overwhelming their main line of resistance. In tactical infantry combat, the Germans managed to keep an edge in firepower over the Red Army until nearly the end of the war. (Author's collection)

A German Panzerjäger crew equipped with the 7.5cm Pak 97/38 anti-tank gun. This weapon was adapted from captured French 75mm Model 1897 guns and relied primarily upon HEAT (High-Explosive Anti-Tank) ammunition, which was still quite novel in 1943. In wooded terrain like this, concealed anti-tank guns could wreak havoc upon attacking enemy tanks. (Author's collection)

Pionier officer in World War I but he had no real experience commanding a large formation. As for the rest of 4.Armee's infantry divisions, their paper strength (*Iststärke*) varied from 9,056 to 16,404 personnel, with an average strength of 11,500 (roughly 68 per cent of authorized strength). However, the actual battle strength (*Gefechtstärke*) of most front-line infantry battalions averaged 375 men, or roughly 45 per cent of their authorized strength. Not only was the quantity of infantry replacements unable to keep up with losses, but the quality of the new troops was often well below previous standards. By mid-1943, Germany was beginning to scrape the lower end of its manpower reserves and the best recruits went to elite units, not infantry units.

Material shortages also undermined the effectiveness of 4.Armee's infantry units. German industry had never been able to fully equip the *Ostheer* with modern German-made weapons and vehicles, which mandated the use of captured French and Soviet equipment as substitutes. For example, only 17 per cent of 4.Armee's machine guns were the excellent MG42, the rest being older MG34s or captured weapons. In terms of anti-tank weapons, nearly half consisted of obsolete 3.7cm Pak or captured Soviet 45mm anti-tank guns. One exception was the army-level Panzerjäger-Abteilung 561, which was equipped with the excellent 7.5cm Pak 41 towed anti-tank guns; in September, this unit was re-equipped with Marder II tank destroyers. Likewise, divisional transport was hindered by the use of a heterogeneous collection of captured motor transport, all of which required different spare parts. Consequently, German infantry divisions were already in a death spiral, with declining manpower, firepower and mobility reducing them to the role of mere 'line holders'.

Artillery

Heeresgruppe Mitte's artillery losses after the retreat from Moscow had never been entirely replaced and Germany's artillery production was inadequate to close the gap. Most of the divisional artillery units in 4.Armee were well below authorized strength. Altogether, the 18 divisions of 4.Armee had about 650 artillery pieces or 77 per cent of their authorized strength. The divisional artillery also included a significant number of captured Czech, French and Soviet weapons. The Heeresartillerie supporting 4.Armee consisted of ten

A German 10.5cm lFH18 gun crew, preparing to fire. In the hot August weather, German artillerymen often stripped down to shorts, but the lack of helmets suggests that they do not expect return fire. Note that the howitzer is not dug in and no other guns are visible. In order to confuse Soviet artillery observers, the Germans in 4.Armee often used single guns to provide local fire support, then later shifted to an alternate position. At the start of *Suvorov*, the Soviets did not know where more than half the German artillery batteries were located. (From Nik Cornish@ Stavka.org.uk)

artillery battalions, equipped with a total of 85 artillery pieces (38 10cm s.K18, 13 15cm s.FH18, nine 15cm K18 and 26 21cm Mörser 18). Heinrici's defence relied heavily upon the artillery and its ability to deliver timely barrages to break up Soviet attacks in the security zone. German artillery units often used mobile batteries that employed 'shoot and move' tactics in order to reduce the effectiveness of enemy counter-battery fire. German artillerymen also had a better idea of where to mass their fires and the enemy was usually exposed in the open; consequently, German defensive artillery fire tended to be more effective than Soviet offensive artillery fire. However, a number of the artillery had worn barrels that had not been replaced, reducing their effectiveness. In addition, 4.Armee did not have adequate stocks of artillery ammunition to fight a prolonged battle.

Armour

At the beginning of August 1943, 4.Armee had negligible armour support. It did have three assault gun battalions with a total of about 60 operational StuG III and StuH 42 assault guns. Some of these assault guns were still equipped with the older, short-barrelled 7.5cm StuK 37 L/24 gun, which made them less useful in the anti-tank role. Initially, the only mobile formation available to 4.Armee was 18.Panzergrenadier-Division but 2.Panzer-Division was in the process of arriving when Operation *Suvorov* began. The 18.Panzergrenadier-Division had suffered crippling losses in the retreat from Moscow in 1941–42 and was never fully restored. By early August 1943, the division had an effective combat strength of 3,000 infantry, 24 artillery pieces and just two assault guns; furthermore, the division only had enough wheeled transport to move one of its infantry regiments at a time. A *Kampfgruppe* from 2.Panzer-Division was transferred from Model's 9.Armee after suffering heavy losses in the Battle of Kursk and arrived with about 20 operational tanks and about one-third of its Panzergrenadiers, but lacked most of its support elements.

A Luftwaffe Fw-190 fighter in autumn 1943. The Fw-190A fighter possessed great firepower and manoeuvrability, but relatively few served on the Eastern Front. In August 1943, the Fw-190s of JG-51 could prevent the Soviet 1st Air Army from achieving air superiority, but the air balance changed for the worse in September. (Bundesarchiv, Bild 101I-664-6789-26A, Foto: Fischer)

After Operation *Suvorov* began, Model was ordered by von Kluge to release additional units to reinforce 4.Armee's sector, but he sent his most depleted formations. During mid-August, Heinrici received 18.Panzer-Division and 25.Panzergrenadier-Division. Both units were severely depleted and arrived piecemeal. The 25.Panzergrenadier Division had 1,170 partially motorized infantry in four battalions, 13 armoured cars and 25 artillery pieces (half of which were Czech-made). The 18.Panzer-Division could only field about 1,200 motorized infantry, 21 artillery pieces and 13 PzKpfw III/IV medium tanks. Heinrici did not receive any Tiger heavy tanks to anchor his defence until Smolensk was threatened in mid-September 1943. In the interim, he had to make do with a hodgepodge of battle-weary PzKpfw III/IV medium tanks and StuG III assault guns, which were too few in number to mount strong mobile counterattacks. By this point in the War in the East, the severely depleted *Panzer-Divisionen* were increasingly reduced to ineffectual detachments rather than fully fledged, combined-arms teams, and were no longer able to dominate the battlefield the way they had in 1941 and 1942.

Aviation

Although Luftflotte 6 only possessed about 350 combat aircraft, it was still an effective fighting force. The three *Jagdgruppen* of JG 51 (equipped with Fw-190A and Bf-109G fighters) based in Bryansk were responsible for counter-air missions over the Smolensk–Roslavl region. Not only was the Fw-190A fighter technically superior to most of the Soviet fighters in this sector of the front, but JG 51 was one of the very best fighter units in the Luftwaffe. At this time, JG 51 included a number of veteran ace pilots, including Oberleutnant Heinrich Höfemeier (96 victories by early August 1943), Oberleutnant Karl-Heinz Weber (85 victories), Major Erich Leie (56 victories) and Leutnant Günther Schack (over 50 victories). In addition, JG 51 had been reinforced by 19 Spanish pilots of 15.Staffel (known as the Blue Squadron or *Escuadrilla Azul*), also flying Fw-190A fighters. The Blue

Heeresgruppe Mitte relied heavily upon the Luftwaffe for ground support, and even in 1943 the Ju-87 Stuka remained capable of delivering punishing dive-bomber attacks on Soviet shock groups. The failure of the VVS to establish air superiority over the main battlefields enabled Stukas to play an important role in breaking up Soviet ground assaults. (From Nik Cornish@ Stavka.org.uk)

Squadron was led by the Spanish ace Major Mariano Cuadra Medina, and this group consisted of well-trained, veteran pilots. However, by the start of *Suvorov*, the pilots of JG 51 had been flying virtually non-stop for a month, both during *Zitadelle* and the attempt to defend the Orel salient, so fatigue was reducing their edge to some extent.

In terms of close air support and battlefield interdiction, Luftflotte 6 was capable of providing up to 350 sorties per day using its three Stuka *Gruppen* and four bomber *Gruppen*. Air strikes were critical in breaking up Soviet assault groups and responding to enemy breakthroughs. In addition, 18.Flak-Division, consisting of 11 battalion-sized units with a total of 585 Flak guns (including 156 8.8cm versions), provided a number of batteries in forward areas; they were usually equipped with a mix of 8.8cm and 2cm Flak guns, which were quite effective against infantry and tank attacks.

Rear-area security

Korück 559 was headquartered in Roslavl and was responsible for protecting the lines of communication behind 4.Armee, as well as providing security in occupied cities. Altogether, Korück 559 comprised 13 German security battalions, four *Ost-Bataillonen* (*Osttruppen* or Eastern volunteers), two light artillery battalions and an assortment of smaller detachments. Heeresgruppe Mitte had also formed a mounted cavalry regiment to help hunt down partisan units in areas that were not accessible by road. Many of the troops in these security units were older reservists or other personnel ill-suited to front-line duty. The Germans were able to form numerous *Osttruppen* security units from former Soviet POWs and local volunteers, but these units were often difficult to control and not capable of conducting effective mobile operations. In practice, Korück 559 relied upon a few battalion-sized mixed *Kampfgruppen* of regular troops to conduct mobile anti-partisan operations, while the rest of its troops were scattered in company-sized garrisons to protect the rail lines and key bridges. Heeresgruppe Mitte had achieved some success in clearing the partisan groups away from the primary line of communication, the Minsk–Moscow Highway, but most of the secondary lines of communication were under regular attack.

ORDERS OF BATTLE

SOVIET

WESTERN FRONT (GENERAL VASILY D. SOKOLOVSKY)

5th Army (General-leytenant Vitaliy S. Polenov)
173rd Rifle Division
207th Rifle Division
208th Rifle Division
312th Rifle Division
352nd Rifle Division
153rd Tank Brigade (42 tanks)
161st Tank Regiment (32 T-34, seven T-70)
1494th Self-Propelled Artillery Regiment (16 SU-122)
3rd Guard Artillery Division

10th Guards Army (General-leytenant Kuzma P. Trubnikov)
7th Guards Rifle Corps
    29th Guards Rifle Division
15th Guards Rifle Corps
    30th Guards Rifle Division
    85th Guards Rifle Division
19th Guards Rifle Corps (General-leytenant Stepan I. Povetkin)
    22nd Guards Rifle Division
    56th Guards Rifle Division
    65th Guards Rifle Division
23rd Guards Tank Brigade (eight KV, 20 T-34, 18 T-70)
119th Tank Regiment (34 T-34)
249th Tank Regiment (four KV, 29 T-34, five T-70)

10th Army (General-leytenant Vasiliy S. Popov)
139th Rifle Division
247th Rifle Division
290th Rifle Division
330th Rifle Division
385th Rifle Division
94th Tank Brigade

21st Army (General-leytenant Nikolai I. Krylov)
61st Rifle Corps
    51st Rifle Division
    62nd Rifle Division
    119th Rifle Division
63rd Rifle Division
70th Rifle Division
76th Rifle Division
95th Rifle Division
174th Rifle Division

31st Army (General-mayor Vladimir A. Gluzdovsky)
36th Rifle Corps (General-mayor Nikolai N. Oleshev)
    215th Rifle Division
    274th Rifle Division
    359th Rifle Division
45th Rifle Corps (General-mayor Stanislav G. Poplavskiy)
    88th Rifle Division
    220th Rifle Division
    331st Rifle Division
71st Rifle Corps
    82nd Rifle Division
    133rd Rifle Division
    251st Rifle Division
42nd Guards Tank Brigade (50 tanks)

33rd Army (General-leytenant Vasily N. Gordov)
42nd Rifle Division
144th Rifle Division
160th Rifle Division
164th Rifle Division
222nd Rifle Division
277th Rifle Division
2nd Guards Tank Brigade

256th Tank Brigade
4th Guards Heavy Cannon Artillery Division

49th Army (General-mayor Ivan T. Grishin)
58th Rifle Division
146th Rifle Division
338th Rifle Division
344th Rifle Division
1537th Self-Propelled Artillery Regiment (12 SU-152)

50th Army (General-leytenant Ivan V. Boldin)
38th Rifle Corps
    17th Rifle Division
    326th Rifle Division
    413th Rifle Division
49th Rifle Division
64th Rifle Division
212th Rifle Division
324th Rifle Division
56th Guards Tank Regiment (31 T-34, six T-70)
233rd Tank Regiment

68th Army (General-leytenant Evgeny P. Zhuralev)
62nd Rifle Corps
    153rd Rifle Division
    154th Rifle Division
    159th Rifle Division
72nd Rifle Corps
    156th Rifle Division
    157th Rifle Division
81st Rifle Corps
    192nd Rifle Division
    199th Rifle Division
120th Tank Brigade (M3 Lee/Matilda/Valentine)
187th Tank Regiment

Western Front Reserves
5th Mechanized Corps (General-leytenant Mikhail V. Volkhov)
    2nd Mechanized Brigade
    9th Mechanized Brigade
    45th Mechanized Brigade
    233rd Tank Brigade
    1827th Self-propelled Artillery Regiment (SU-152)
6th Guards Cavalry Corps (General-major Sergei V. Sokolov)
    8th Guards Cavalry Division
    13th Guards Cavalry Division
    8th Cavalry Division
70th Rifle Corps
    317th Rifle Division
    36th Rifle Brigade
5th Breakthrough Artillery Corps (General-mayor Mikhail P. Kuteinikov)
    7th Guards Mortar Division (M-31)
43rd Guards Tank Brigade
213th Tank Brigade
63rd Guards Tank Regiment (21 KV)

1st Air Army (General-leytenant Mikhail M. Gromov)
2nd Bombing Aviation Corps
    223rd Bomber Aviation Division
    10th Bomber Aviation Regiment (Pe-2)
    285th Bomber Aviation Division
    150th Bomber Aviation Regiment (Pe-2)
    205th Bomber Aviation Regiment (Pe-2)
2nd Assault Aviation Corps
    231st Ground Attack Aviation Division
    568th Ground Attack Aviation Regiment (Il-2)
    570th Ground Attack Aviation Regiment (Il-2)
    873rd Ground Attack Aviation Regiment (Il-2)
    232nd Ground Attack Aviation Division
    230th Ground Attack Aviation Regiment (Il-2)

704th Ground Attack Aviation Regiment (Il-2)
801st Ground Attack Aviation Regiment (Il-2)
2nd Fighter Aviation Corps
  7th Guards Fighter Aviation Division
    1st Guards Fighter Aviation Regiment
    89th Guards Fighter Aviation Regiment
    146th Fighter Aviation Regiment (Yak-7)
  322nd Fighter Aviation Division
    2nd Guards Fighter Aviation Regiment
    482nd Fighter Aviation Regiment (La-5)
    937th Fighter Aviation Regiment (La-5)
8th Fighter Aviation Corps
  215th Fighter Aviation Division
    263rd Fighter Aviation Regiment (La-5)
    522nd Fighter Aviation Regiment (La-5)
    813th Fighter Aviation Regiment (La-5)
  323rd Fighter Aviation Division
    149th Fighter Aviation Regiment (Yak-7)
    484th Fighter Aviation Regiment (Yak-7)
    518th Fighter Aviation Regiment (Yak-7)
11th Composite Air Corps
  4th Fighter Aviation Regiment (Yak-9)
  148th Fighter Aviation Regiment (Yak-9)
  293rd Fighter Aviation Regiment (Yak-9)
  724th Ground Attack Aviation Regiment (Il-2)
204th Bomber Aviation Division
  2nd Bomber Aviation Regiment (Pe-2)
  6th Bomber Aviation Regiment (Pe-2)
  38th Bomber Aviation Regiment (Pe-2)
  130th Bomber Aviation Regiment (Pe-2)
  261st Bomber Aviation Regiment (Pe-2)
224th Ground Attack Aviation Division
  565th Ground Attack Aviation Regiment (Il-2)
  566th Ground Attack Aviation Regiment (Il-2)
  571st Ground Attack Aviation Regiment (Il-2)
  996th Ground Attack Aviation Regiment (Il-2)
  513th Fighter Aviation Regiment (Yak-1)
233rd Ground Attack Aviation Division
  62nd Ground Attack Aviation Regiment (Il-2)
  198th Ground Attack Aviation Regiment (Il-2)
  312th Ground Attack Aviation Regiment (Il-2)
  122nd Fighter Aviation Regiment (Yak-7b)
311th Ground Attack Aviation Division
  952nd Ground Attack Aviation Regiment (Il-2)
  953rd Ground Attack Aviation Regiment (Il-2)
  956th Ground Attack Aviation Regiment (Il-2)
303rd Fighter Aviation Division
  18th Guards Fighter Aviation Regiment (Yak-7b)
  20th Fighter Aviation Regiment (Yak-9)
  168th Fighter Aviation Regiment (Yak-7)
  494th Fighter Aviation Regiment (P-39)
309th Fighter Aviation Division
  49th Fighter Aviation Regiment (La-5)
  272nd Fighter Aviation Regiment (La-5)
  162nd Fighter Aviation Regiment (Yak-7b)
  172nd Fighter Aviation Regiment (Yak-7b)
213th Night Bomber Aviation Division
  24th Guards Night Bomber Aviation Regiment (Po-2)
  15th Night Bomber Aviation Regiment (Po-2)
  16th Night Bomber Aviation Regiment (Po-2)
  17th Night Bomber Aviation Regiment (Po-2)
  615th Night Bomber Aviation Regiment (Po-2)
  634th Night Bomber Aviation Regiment (Po-2)
  644th Night Bomber Aviation Regiment (Po-2)

Soviet aircraft numbers

Type (est.)	Number operational (est.)	Total on hand
Fighter	460	675
Bomber	135	200
Ground Attack	400	450
Night Bomber	50	90
Total	**1,045**	**1,415**

KALININ FRONT (GENERAL-POLKOVNIK ANDREI I. EREMENKO)

39th Army (General-leytenant Aleksei I. Zygin)[1]
2nd Guards Rifle Corps (General-leytenant Afanasy P. Beloborodov)
  9th Guards Rifle Division
  17th Guards Rifle Division
  91st Guards Rifle Division
83rd Rifle Corps
  178th Rifle Division
  185th Rifle Division
  124th Rifle Brigade
84th Rifle Corps (General-leytenant Sergei A. Knyazkov)
  134th Rifle Division
  158th Rifle Division
  234th Rifle Division
21st Artillery Division
28th Guards Tank Brigade
143rd Tank Brigade (T-34)
11th Guards Tank Regiment (21 KV-1)
203rd Tank Regiment
43rd Army (General-leytenant Konstantin D. Golubev)
145th Rifle Division
179th Rifle Division
262nd Rifle Division
306th Rifle Division
114th Rifle Brigade
105th Tank Regiment
Kalinin Front Reserves
3rd Guards Cavalry Corps (General-mayor Nikolai S. Oslikovsky)
  5th Guards Cavalry Division
  6th Guards Cavalry Division
  32nd Cavalry Division
8th Rifle Corps
  7th Rifle Division
  249th Rifle Division
Mobile Group of Kalinin Front (Polkovnik Ivan. F. Dremov)
  28th Guards Tank Brigade (58 T-34, 14 T-70, 16 Su-122)
  46th Mechanized Brigade
  47th Mechanized Brigade
Tank Group Chuprova
  60th Tank Brigade
  236th Tank Brigade
221st Tank Regiment (32 T-34, seven T-70)
3rd Air Army (General-mayor Nikolai F. Papivin)
211th Ground Attack Aviation Division
  723rd Ground Attack Aviation Regiment (Il-2)
  826th Ground Attack Aviation Regiment (Il-2)
  949th Ground Attack Aviation Regiment (Il-2)
6th Guards Attack Aviation Regiment (Il-2)
259th Fighter Aviation Division
  21st (La-5) Fighter Aviation Regiment
  761st (Yak-7b) Fighter Aviation Regiment

---

1 Zygin was replaced by General-leytenant Nikolai E. Berzarin on 9 September 1943.

GERMAN

HEERESGRUPPE MITTE (GENERALFELDMARSCHALL GÜNTHER VON KLUGE)

4.Armee (Generaloberst Gotthard Heinrici)
XXVII Armeekorps (General der Infanterie Paul Völckers)
    52.Infanterie-Division
    197.Infanterie-Division
    246.Infanterie-Division
    256.Infanterie-Division
    Sturmgeschütz-Abteilung 237
XXXIX Panzerkorps (General der Artillerie Robert Martinek)
    18.Panzergrenadier-Division
    35.Infanterie-Division
    113.Infanterie-Division
    337.Infanterie-Division
    Sturmgeschütz-Abteilung 185
IX Armeekorps (General der Infanterie Hans Schmidt)
    252.Infanterie-Division
    342.Infanterie-Division
    2./Sturmgeschütz-Abteilung 667
XII Armeekorps (General der Infanterie Kurt von Tippelskirch)
    260.Infanterie-Division
    267.Infanterie-Division
    268.Infanterie-Division
    3./Sturmgeschütz-Abteilung 667
LVI Panzerkorps (General der Infanterie Friedrich Hossbach)
    14.Infanterie-Division (mot.)
    131.Infanterie-Division
    321.Infanterie-Division
Army Reserve
    Kampfgruppe/56.Infanterie-Division (five infantry battalions)
    36.Infanterie-Division (mot.)

Korück 559
Sicherungs-Bataillon 222
Sicherungs-Bataillon 555
Sicherungs-Bataillon 557
Sicherungs-Bataillon 684
Sicherungs-Bataillon 787
Sicherungs-Bataillon 810
Landesschützen-Bataillon 675
Landesschützen-Bataillon 826
Wach-Bataillon 551
Wach-Bataillon 582
Radfahr-Wach-Bataillon 50
Feldgendarmerie-Abteilung 697
Kavallerie-Regiment Mitte (Major Georg Freiherr von Boeselager)

Luftflotte 6 (Generaloberst Robert Ritter von Greim)
4.Flieger Division (Generalleutnant Hermann Plocher)[2]
    I, III./Jagdgeschwader 51 (72 Fw-190A)
    IV./Jagdgeschwader 51 (35 Bf-109G)
    15.(Span.)/Jagdgeschwader 51 (17 Fw-190A)
    III./Kampfgeschwader 1 (18 Ju-88A)
    Stab., II., III./Kampfgeschwader 4 (74 He-111)
    II./Kampfgeschwader 51 (37 Ju-88A)
    Stab., I., II., III./Sturzkampfgeschwader 1 (four Bf-110E/G, 96 Ju-87D)

18.Flak-Division (Generalleutnant Prinz Heinrich Reuss)
Flak-Regiment 6 (mot.)
    II./Flak-Regiment 26
    II./Flak-Regiment 49, leichte
    Flak-Abteilung 93 (Sfl.)
Flak-Regiment 10 (mot.)
    II./Flak-Regiment 4
    I./Flak-Regiment 29
    I./Flak-Regiment 52
    I./Flak-Regiment 704, leichte
    Flak-Abteilung 94 (Sfl.)
Flak-Regiment 35 (mot.)
    II./Flak-Regiment 11
    I./Flak-Regiment 36 leichte
    Flak-Abteilung 83 (Sfl.)

German aircraft numbers

Type	Number operational (est.)	Total on hand
Fighter	100	138
Bomber	95	129
Ground attack	70	96
Total	**265**	**363**

Reinforcements
8 August 1943
    2.Panzer-Division
10 August 1943
    9.Panzer-Division[3]
13 August 1943
    18.Panzer-Division
    25.Panzergrenadier-Division
14 August 1943
    20.Panzer-Division[4]
16 August
    Sturm-Regiment AOK 4[5]
31 August 1943
    1.SS-Infanterie Brigade (mot.)[6] (SS-Brigadeführer Karl Herrmann)
    Sturmgeschütz-Abteilung 190
1 September 1943
    330.Infanterie-Division
    schwere Panzerjäger-Abteilung 655 (40 Hornisse)
17 September 1943
    schwere Panzer-Abteilung 505 (Tiger)

---

3 Transferred to Panzerarmee 2 in late August.
4 Transferred to Panzerarmee 2 in late August.
5 An ad hoc unit formed on 16 August 1943 from training personnel. It initially consisted of two infantry battalions and was later expanded to three.
6 This Waffen-SS unit consisted of four motorized infantry battalions, a light artillery battalion, an assault gun battery and various support units. It was attached to 25.Panzergrenadier-Division.

2 On 25 August, Plocher was replaced by Oberst Franz Reuss.

The situation in the Smolensk sector, 6 August 1943

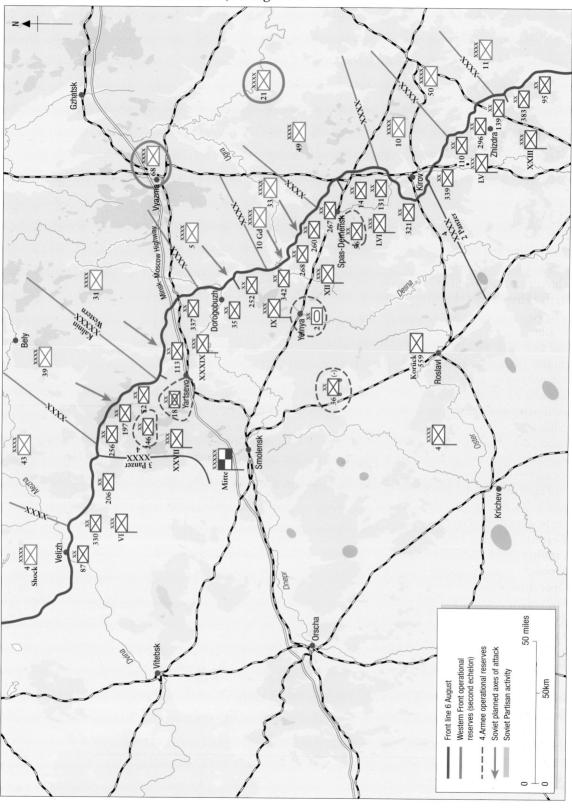

OPPOSING PLANS

SOVIET

On the evening of 12 April, Zhukov met with Stalin and other members of Stavka in the Kremlin in order to discuss future operational plans. Both Zhukov and Marshal Aleksandr M. Vasilevsky (chief of the Soviet General Staff) believed that the Germans intended to attack both sides of the Soviet-held Kursk salient, but argued that it would be better for the Red Army to allow the Germans to exhaust their best *Panzer-Divisionen* on the thick anti-tank defences being emplaced there. Unlike 1942, the Red Army had amassed a considerable numerical superiority over the enemy and its tactics had noticeably improved, which made it unlikely that the German offensive would achieve its objectives. Zhukov and Vasilevsky recommended waiting until after the German offensive had spent itself and their reserves were exhausted before launching a carefully planned riposte by the Red Army. For once, Stalin was swayed by the arguments of his military professionals and agreed to authorize a temporary shift to defensive operations until Operation *Zitadelle* had been repulsed. Then the Red Army would have its day.

From mid-April, Stavka began planning a series of multi-front counter-offensives that were intended to throw the German invaders back on their heels. Once the German offensive against the Kursk salient ended, the Western, Bryansk and Central fronts would conduct Operation *Kutusov*, a multi-pronged counter-offensive intended to eliminate the Orel salient. Around the same time, the Voronezh and Steppe fronts would launch Operation *Rumyantsev* to liberate Kharkov and set the stage for a drive towards the Dnepr. Soon afterwards, the Western and Kalinin fronts would begin Operation *Suvorov*, with the intent of liberating Bryansk and Smolensk. Other supporting offensives were planned at Leningrad, in the Donbass and in the Kuban. Eleven of the 12 active Soviet fronts would be involved in the summer offensives planned by Stavka, leaving only the North-West Front on the sidelines. Stavka wanted to gain and maintain the strategic initiative by inflicting multiple blows upon various sectors of the German front, hoping to cause a collapse wherever possible. Furthermore, by attacking all four German army groups nearly simultaneously, the enemy would find it more difficult to transfer reserves from one sector to another. However, even with increased Lend-Lease aid from the Anglo-Americans, the Red Army would be hard-pressed to logistically support all these simultaneous offensives.

After developing the broad objectives for Operation *Suvorov*, in June 1943 Stavka assigned the primary responsibility for detailed tactical planning to the Western Front, with the Kalinin Front playing only a supporting role. Since the Western Front was also involved in planning its role in Operation *Kutusov*, its staff was burdened with simultaneously preparing for two major operations. General-leytenant Aleksandr P. Pokrovsky, chief of staff of the Western Front, was one of the most experienced general staff-trained officers in the Red Army, having served with the Western Front since the Battle of Smolensk in 1941. However, Soviet fronts did not have large organic staffs like Western armies and Pokrovsky's small cadre of staff officers was stretched to the limit just to coordinate critical operations, intelligence and logistic functions. Secondary tasks, including coordination with the VVS to arrange air support and *maskirovka* (deception), were given only perfunctory attention. Nor did the Western Front possess a good understanding of the enemy order of battle in their sector. Polkovnik Yakov T. Ilnitsky, head of the Western Front's intelligence section, relied too heavily on prisoner interrogations for basic tactical information and failed to coordinate aerial reconnaissance and signals collection. Soviet partisan units might have helped gather information on German unit transfers, but they had very few radios and were focused on attacking rail lines, not intelligence collection.

As designed by Stavka, the basic concept for Operation *Suvorov* was for the Western Front to make the main effort against the German 4.Armee along the Spas-Demensk–Roslavl axis. Meanwhile, the Kalinin Front would mount a supporting attack against 4.Armee's left flank, north of Smolensk. The initial objective of the offensive was to drive a deep wedge into the centre of Heeresgruppe Mitte by capturing Roslavl, then pivot north to crush the German defenders in Smolensk between the pincers of the Western and Kalinin fronts. The planners ambitiously hoped to continue the offensive westwards after Smolensk was liberated, but no specific follow-on objectives were stated. Like the other Soviet counter-offensives being planned, *Suvorov* was intended to be a carefully prepared and conducted operation, unlike the ad hoc attacks in 1941–42. General Vasily D. Sokolovsky, the new commander of the Western Front, also favoured a methodical approach, hoping to avoid another Operation *Mars*. Pokrovsky knew from previous failed offensives that 4.Armee's defences would be difficult to breach, so it was decided to attack in two echelons, each with two infantry armies. Rather than committing everything up front, Pokrovsky wanted to be able to feed fresh forces into the battle, thereby maintaining momentum. Three armies – the 11th, 21st and 68th – were transferred from the Stavka reserves to reinforce the Western Front.

Soviet signalmen stringing communications wire across a water obstacle. The area in which the Soviet offensive occurred was criss-crossed by numerous water obstacles, which affected both mobility and communications. The Red Army preferred wire communications at the tactical level because they were usually more secure than radio communications, but this required a continuous effort to maintain signal lines. (Courtesy of the Central Museum of the Armed Forces, Moscow via www.Stavka.org.uk)

Unlike Zhukov's offensives against Heeresgruppe Mitte in 1942, the Western Front was provided much less armour (most of which had gone to the Central, Voronezh and Steppe fronts) for Operation *Suvorov*. Furthermore, all four of the tank corps belonging to the Western Front were committed to Operation *Kutusov* by mid-July, so the 5th Mechanized Corps was transferred to give Sokolovsky a formation large enough to form a front-level mobile group. Yet given the nature of the heavily wooded terrain and depth of the enemy defences, Sokolovsky and Pokrovsky were aware that large armoured formations would be difficult to employ and instead intended to use most of their armour in the infantry support role to reduce enemy strongpoints. Unlike Zhukov, Sokolovsky had no intention of risking his mechanized spearheads being cut off and destroyed by German counterattacks. In addition, the Western Front and Kalinin Front still had substantial cavalry formations available to exploit any local successes, particularly in wooded areas. Sokolovsky was provided with ample artillery for the offensive, but due to the priority of other front-level operations, Stavka only sent enough ammunition to support the initial breakthrough battles. In another mark of improved planning, Stavka provided the Western Front with four assault engineer brigades to assist in obstacle clearing.

The timing of Operation *Suvorov* was dependent upon the progress achieved by the Bryansk Front and the Western Front's 11th Guards Army in Operation *Kutusov*. Ideally, Heeresgruppe Mitte's right flank would be destabilized by the earlier operation and in retreat before the Western Front began its push towards Roslavl. Soviet intelligence on 4.Armee's front-line defences was adequate, but there was little information on the location or size of enemy mobile reserves. Overall, Operation *Suvorov* was a cautious offensive, intended to secure significant territorial objectives but without making the kind of tactical mistakes made during Operation *Mars*. In essence, the operation exemplified the Soviet mantra of 'probing with bayonets in order to find a weak spot', but lacked the resources or imagination that could lead to rapid, decisive success.

A German assault gun unit arrives at the Orscha train station in August 1943. Heeresgruppe Mitte was aware of the impending Soviet offensive against 4.Armee and tried to reinforce Heinrici with armoured units taken from Model's 9.Armee. (Süddeutsche Zeitung Bild 00094548, Foto: Germin)

GERMAN

Heeresgruppe Mitte's primary mission was defensive in nature, to hold key terrain while not making demands upon other fronts for reinforcements. Nevertheless, von Kluge continued to plan for limited-scale offensive operations to be conducted at the right moment. Since January 1943, he had intended to eliminate the Soviet-held Kirov salient with a pincer attack when the required two *Panzer-Divisionen* became available, but this effort was continually postponed. Von Kluge also had to contend with large partisan bands that operated in his rear areas and harassed his supply lines. Consequently, 4.Armee and the rear area command Korück 559 were obliged to regularly mount large-scale anti-partisan operations such as Operation *Nachbarhilfe* and *Wintersturm*.

In the 4.Armee sector, Heinrici established multiple lines of defence. At the front, a heavily reinforced security zone was protected by mines, anti-tank ditches and wire obstacles, while the troops occupied consecutive trench lines. One particularly important position was the Büffel-Stellung (Buffalo position) located near the village of Gnezdilovo and held by 260. Infanterie-Division. On the left flank of 4.Armee, XXVII Armeekorps held the strongly fortified Barbarossa-Stellung. While not impregnable, Heinrici's defences were formidable. Each infantry regiment typically had two of its three battalions up front, each holding a 2km-wide sector. The main German line of resistance, the *Hauptkampflinie* (HKL), was about 3–4km back from the front and held by reserve battalions. The Germans were also aided by the fact that the heavily wooded and marshy terrain in this region favoured the defence, providing ample cover and concealment for positions – making it more difficult for the Soviets to pinpoint their HKL or artillery. In particular, the Germans used nearly half their batteries in a mobile role, shooting and then shifting to alternate positions, which made it difficult for Soviet intelligence to pinpoint them. Even on a quiet day, a typical front-line German division was still firing 15 tons of artillery ammunition.

A German Flak unit passes through Smolensk in June 1943. Although the Germans had drafted local civilians for forced labour in Germany, there was still a significant population in Smolensk in mid-1943. However, as the Red Army moved closer to the city, the Germans acted to remove anyone who might eventually benefit the Soviet war effort. (Bundesarchiv, Bild 183-J14678, Foto: Werner Spitta)

Although the spring season was relatively quiet, Heinrici knew that the Western Front would eventually mount a major effort towards Smolensk. On 25 June, 4.Armee issued an order that Smolensk would be turned into a fortress. Oberst Schmidt from Pionier-Regiments-Stab z.b.V. 628 was put in charge of Pionier-Regiments-Stab Smolensk and tasked with completing a defensive ring around the city within three months. Schmidt had several *Bau-Bataillone* (construction battalions), as well as 2,500 local civilians. The defences consisted of trenches, barbed wire, and a few bunkers, some of which were completed before Operation *Suvorov* began.

Von Kluge knew that he would have far less air and armour support to counter the next enemy offensive than he had enjoyed in 1942. Instead, he had to rely upon more rigid defensive tactics and hope that any Soviet offensives could be fought to a stalemate before he expended his limited reserves. Unlike their Soviet counterparts, both Heeresgruppe Mitte and 4.Armee had large, well-trained staffs who knew how to make the best of available resources. The Germans also benefitted from the Western Front's ineffective *maskirovka* efforts, which enabled 4.Armee's intelligence officer, Oberstleutnant Jobst von Reden, to accurately predict that the enemy was likely to attack in the XII Armeekorps sector near Spas-Demensk and in the XXXIX Panzerkorps sector near Dorogobuzh. Von Kluge had nearly a week's warning time before *Suvorov* began, which enabled him to reposition his limited reserves. The 18.Panzergrenadier-Division and two assault gun battalions were placed in tactical reserve behind XXXIX Panzerkorps. Given that Model's 9.Armee was evacuating the Orel salient and falling back to the Hagen-Stellung, von Kluge was able to get 2.Panzer-Division and two depleted infantry divisions (36 and 56) released to reinforce 4.Armee prior to the start of *Suvorov*. Consequently, the Germans had a fairly good idea where and when Operation *Suvorov* was likely to strike and were able to adjust their defences in the threatened sectors before Sokolovsky landed a single blow.

THE CAMPAIGN

PRELIMINARY MOVES, 1–6 AUGUST 1943

By the beginning of August, von Kluge knew that a major offensive by the Western Front was imminent and three of Model's divisions were in the process of transferring to reinforce 4.Armee. On 3 August, Soviet partisans began Operation *Rail War*, blowing up numerous sections of railway tracks, particularly west of Smolensk and around Orscha, Krichev and Mogilev. Although the attacks did not immediately impact Heeresgruppe Mitte's logistics, Soviet partisan attacks did introduce an element of friction that hindered German supply operations and unit transfers. However, neither Soviet partisans nor the lacklustre VVS reconnaissance effort detected the transfer of divisions to reinforce 4.Armee. Gromov's 1st Air Army attempted to bomb German rail lines near Smolensk and Roslavl, but the Fw-190A fighters of Jagdgeschwader 51 made deep raids costly. During the first five days of August, Jagdgeschwader 51 claimed no fewer than 211 victories, including ten Pe-2 and 11 Boston bombers claimed on 5 August, for the loss of just seven of their own fighters. Even assuming the normal over-claiming, it is clear that 1st Air Army suffered heavy losses before *Suvorov* even began.

Stalin also made a rare visit to the front four days before the operation began to personally discuss Operation *Suvorov* with both Sokolovsky and Eremenko. He arrived at the Western Front's rear command post near Yukhnov on 3 August. Stalin was interested in operational details and preparations for the offensive. No doubt Stalin's visit was unnerving for Sokolovsky and his staff, particularly when General-polkovnik Kamera had the temerity to complain to Stalin about the insufficient amount of artillery ammunition provided. Stalin curtly replied that Stavka had no more to provide at the moment and the front would have to make do with its available stockpile. Stalin's visit let Sokolovsky know that the Kremlin leadership would be closely following the campaign and that failures like Operation *Mars* would not be tolerated.

On 6 August, the Western Front began probing attacks in the sectors of the 5th, 33rd and 10th armies. In modern terms, this phase would be called the 'counter-reconnaissance battle', with one side trying to get more specific information on enemy dispositions and the other trying to deny it. The German security zone was generally about 2–3km deep, with platoon-sized outposts covering likely avenues of approach, which were blocked with obstacles and covered by artillery. Each of the Soviet first-echelon assault divisions committed an advance guard battalion, supported by artillery and a few tanks, to advancing into the German security zones. German resistance in the IX and XII Armeekorps sectors proved stiff and the Soviet infantry was not able to occupy much ground. In the 268.Infanterie-Division sector, a probe by the 3rd Battalion/1295th Rifle Regiment was repulsed with 150 killed and 18 captured; under interrogation, one of the Russian prisoners revealed the start time of the Soviet offensive. The Western Front also conducted aggressive probing in other sectors, in an effort to deceive the Germans where the main attacks would occur. The Kalinin Front's 39th Army also probed the outer defences of the German XXVII Armeekorps, but Heinrici knew this was a feint. By the end of the day, not only had 4.Armee's front-line outpost lines prevented Sokolovsky's advance battalions from reaching anywhere near the main German HKLs, but the Soviets had squandered all tactical surprise. At dusk on 6 August, Luftflotte 6 launched bomber raids against suspected enemy assembly areas, which were also harassed with long-range artillery fire during the night.

THE OPENING ROUND, 7–21 AUGUST 1943

At 0440hrs on 7 August, Kamera's artillery began its preparation barrage with a 10-minute fire-strike against the forward German outposts. Then, the barrage shifted further back, pounding the suspected main German positions for nearly an hour. After this, the ADD conducted a 10-minute counter-battery barrage against suspected German artillery positions, followed by a final suppression barrage against the enemy front line. In less than two hours, Kamera expended more than 50 per cent of his available ammunition. Then at 0630hrs, the artillery barrage abated and the Soviet ground attacks began immediately. The weather was hot (77° F/25° C) and muggy, and the skies were cloudless.

In the Dorogobuzh sector, General-leytenant Vitaliy S. Polenov's 5th Army attacked with the 207th, 208th and 352nd Rifle divisions, the 153rd Tank Brigade and 161st Tank Regiment. The main blow fell on Generalleutnant Walter Melzer's 252.Infanterie-Division from IX Armeekorps, which was bombarded with roughly 50,000 Soviet artillery rounds. Leutnant Armin Scheiderbauer recalled, 'Only seconds after the barrage had finished, you could hear small arms fire. Through the clear sounds of the Russian sub-

In addition to shortages of fuel and ammunition, the troops of the Western and Kalinin fronts were tormented by recurrent food shortages, which led to widespread malnutrition in front-line units. Soviet troops were supposed to receive a daily ration of 800g of black bread, 150g of meat and 500g of vegetables, but meat was rare until US Lend-Lease beef began to arrive in quantity. Most Soviet troops subsisted on *kacha*, a wheat stew, and whatever odds and ends the rear services allowed to reach the front. (Author's collection)

A Soviet rifle squad waits for a bombardment to lift. This squad is armed with a mix of rifles, PPS-41 sub-machine guns and DP light machine guns, and the troops appear to be veterans. (Author's collection)

machine guns came the chattering of machine guns belonging to our lads.' The Soviet attacks made only slight advances, due to heavy German defensive fire. A motorized Panzerjäger detachment succeeded in knocking out many of the supporting Soviet tanks and local counterattacks recovered the ground that had been lost. Nevertheless, 252.Infanterie-Division suffered 376 casualties on the first day of the enemy offensive and the rate of losses remained high on subsequent days.

The Western Front's main effort was made between Yelnya and Spas-Demensk by General-leytenant Kuzma P. Trubnikov's 10th Guards Army and General-leytenant Vasily N. Gordov's 33rd Army. On the right, Trubnikov committed the 15th Guards Rifle Corps (30th Guards Rifle Division, 85th Guards Rifle Division) and 19th Guards Rifle Corps (56th Guards Rifle Division, 65th Guards Rifle Division) into a 10km wide sector between Mazovo and Sluzna; he kept two more rifle divisions in reserve. In addition, Volkhov's 5th Mechanized Corps was assembled behind the 10th Guards Army, ready to exploit the expected breakthrough. Trubnikov's operational objective for the first day of the offensive was the town of Pavlinovo, situated on the Smolensk–Spas-Demensk railway, 10km to the south. The German defence in this sector rested upon the Büffel-Stellung position, held by XII Armeekorps. Generalleutnant Walther Hahm's 260.Infanterie-Division (Grenadier-Regiment 460, Grenadier-Regiment 480) and Generalleutnant Heinrich Greiner's 268.Infanterie-Division (Grenadier-Regiment 488 and Grenadier-Regiment 499) had both been reduced to just two infantry regiments and were assigned very wide sectors. Although the German divisions were outnumbered by more than 3:1, the terrain was heavily wooded and dotted with numerous villages, all of which were fortified. Even worse, Soviet intelligence had failed to identify the key German positions, centred upon the villages of Gnezdilovo and the nearby Hill 233.3, held by Oberst Lothar Ambrosius' Grenadier-Regiment 488. Indeed, the Germans had prepared elaborate defences atop Hill 233.3, surrounded by barbed wire, anti-tank ditches and dense minefields – none of which had even been scratched by the preparatory bombardment.

Shortly after crossing the line of departure, General-leytenant Stepan I. Povetkin's 19th Guards Rifle Corps encountered heavy resistance from Oberst Franz Linding's Grenadier-Regiment 499. Typically, each front-line German infantry company was attacked by a pair of Soviet rifle battalions. However, Greiner used his efficient divisional artillery to break up the enemy assault groups before they could make any progress, while a pair of assault guns from 3./Sturmgeschütz-Abteilung 667 picked off advancing T-34s from the 119th Tank Regiment. The German resistance between Kamenka and Sluzna was so strong that the Soviet assault groups from the 56th Guards Rifle Division and 65th Guards Rifle Division were disrupted and barely able to advance, but here and there, some small fragments found a way through.

Guards Lieutenant Aleksei V. Sosnovsky, a platoon commander from the 257th Guards Rifle Regiment, managed to penetrate into one German position with just six soldiers and overran an enemy mortar detachment. However, no further Soviet troops followed Sosnovsky and his small group was soon isolated and eliminated by a German counterattack. In the final hand-to-hand fighting, Sosnovsky blew himself up with a grenade; he was later posthumously awarded the Hero of the Soviet Union. Nearby, Leytenant Ivan S. Povoroznyuk, a platoon leader in the 119th Tank Regiment, also succeeded in getting close enough with his T-34 to knock out some German infantry positions. Although the 56th Guards Rifle Division managed to carve out a 1km-deep penetration near Kamenka, it was evident that the 19th Guards Rifle Corps attack had been stopped cold. The 15th Guards Rifle Corps attacked around 1000hrs and achieved some success, slowing pushing back Linding's Grenadier-Regiment 499.

Meanwhile, Gordov's 33rd Army attacked with three rifle divisions (42nd, 160th and 164th) and the 256th Tank Brigade on the eastern flank of the Büffel-Stellung, but also ran into tough resistance from Grenadier-Regiment 480 in the Kurkino sector. Only a limited success was achieved by the 164th Rifle Division, which captured the village of Chotilovka and threatened to drive a wedge into the front between Grenadier-Regiment 460 and Grenadier-Regiment 480. However, Hauptman Hans Hemling's II./Grenadier-Regiment 480 stopped any further advance. By early afternoon on 7 August, Sokolovsky became concerned about the inability of most of his units to advance and arbitrarily relieved the commander of the 65th Guards Rifle Division. He also decided to commit part of his second echelon force – General-leytenant Evgeny P. Zhuralev's 68th Army – to reinforce the push by Trubnikov's 10th Guards Army against XII Armeekorps. This was a premature and foolish decision on a number of levels, crowding an already stalled front with even more troops and vehicles, which did not lead to any immediate success. Nevertheless, the tide of Soviet manpower began to surge

ASSAULT ON THE BÜFFEL-STELLUNG, 7–10 AUGUST 1943

Trubnikov's 10th Guards Army tried repeatedly to smash through XII Armeekorps' defensive lines, which were anchored by a strong point on Hill 233.3 near the village of Gnezdilovo. The Germans kept feeding in reinforcements from 9.Armee to plug weak spots in the line. With help from the 33rd Army, Trubnikov's divisions finally began to wear down the German defence after four days of fighting.

SOVIET
1. 164th Rifle Division (33rd Army)
2. 65th Guards Rifle Division and 119th Tank Regiment
3. 56th Guards Rifle Division and 249th Tank Regiment
4. 85th Guards Rifle Division
5. 81st Rifle Corps (68th Army)
6. 29th Guards Rifle Division and 23rd Tank Brigade

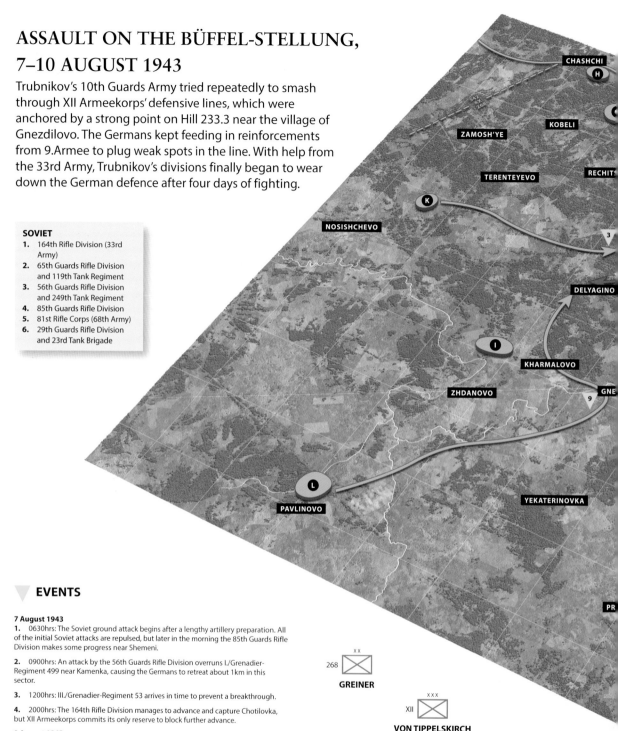

CHASHCHI
ZAMOSH'YE
KOBELI
TERENTEYEVO
RECHIT
NOSISHCHEVO
DELYAGINO
KHARMALOVO
ZHDANOVO
GNE
YEKATERINOVKA
PAVLINOVO
PR

268
X X
GREINER

XII
X X X
VON TIPPELSKIRCH

▼ EVENTS

7 August 1943
1. 0630hrs: The Soviet ground attack begins after a lengthy artillery preparation. All of the initial Soviet attacks are repulsed, but later in the morning the 85th Guards Rifle Division makes some progress near Shemeni.

2. 0900hrs: An attack by the 56th Guards Rifle Division overruns I./Grenadier-Regiment 499 near Kamenka, causing the Germans to retreat about 1km in this sector.

3. 1200hrs: III./Grenadier-Regiment 53 arrives in time to prevent a breakthrough.

4. 2000hrs: The 164th Rifle Division manages to advance and capture Chotilovka, but XII Armeekorps commits its only reserve to block further advance.

8 August 1943
5. 0730hrs: The 65th Guards Rifle Division captures Veselukha, but its efforts to storm Hill 233.3 are repulsed.

6. 0830–1120hrs: The 164th Rifle Division attacks towards Sluzna, in an effort to outflank the defences on Hill 233.3.

7. Morning: The 81st Rifle Corps from 68th Army is committed to reinforce the attack upon 268.Infanterie-Division's left flank, which initially makes minimal progress.

8. Night 8/9 August: The Germans evacuate Sluzna in order to avoid encirclement, but form a new line of resistance, which blocks further efforts by the 164th Rifle Division to advance.

9 August 1943
9. 0800hrs: A *Kampfgruppe* from 2.Panzer-Division arrives to reinforce the German position around Delyagino.

10. 1030–1430hrs: Further attacks by the 65th Guards Rifle Division on Hill 233.3 are repulsed.

10 August 1943
11. 1330hrs: The 56th Guards Rifle Division attacks the Delyagino position and finally captures the village, causing the Germans to retire 2km to the south.

12. 1500hrs: The 29th Guards Rifle Division and 23rd Tank Brigade attack and finally capture Hill 233.3 after six hours of fighting.

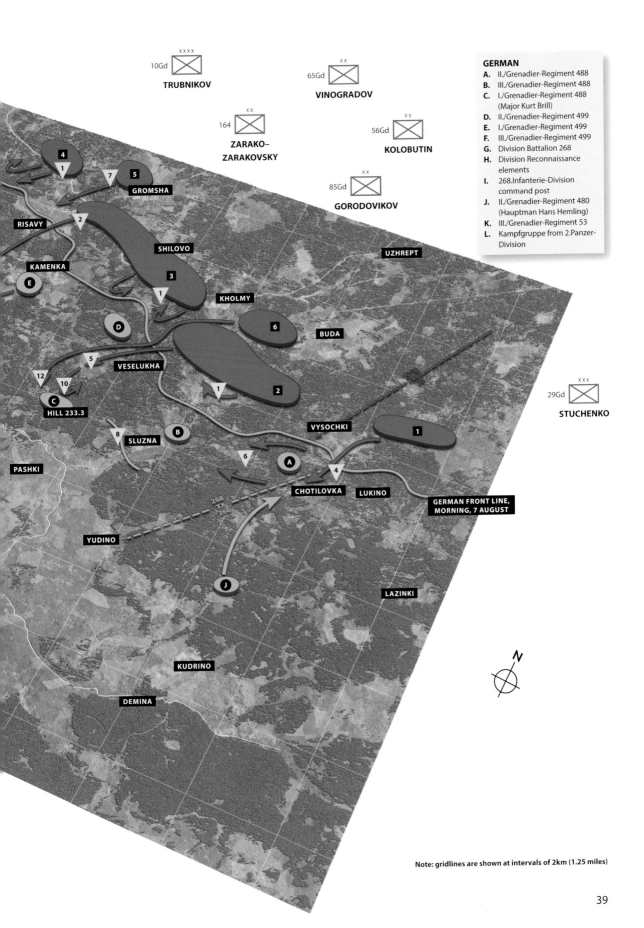

10Gd
TRUBNIKOV

65Gd
VINOGRADOV

164
**ZARAKO–
ZARAKOVSKY**

56Gd
KOLOBUTIN

85Gd
GORODOVIKOV

29Gd
STUCHENKO

4
1

7   5

GROMSHA

2

RISAVY

SHILOVO

3

1

KAMENKA

E

KHOLMY

6

D

BUDA

5

VESELUKHA

12

10

1

C

2

HILL 233.3

VYSOCHKI

8

1

SLUZNA

B

6

A

4

PASHKI

268
XX
266

CHOTILOVKA   **LUKINO**

UZHREPT

**GERMAN FRONT LINE,
MORNING, 7 AUGUST**

YUDINO

J

LAZINKI

KUDRINO

DEMINA

N

GERMAN
A. II./Grenadier-Regiment 488
B. III./Grenadier-Regiment 488
C. I./Grenadier-Regiment 488
   (Major Kurt Brill)
D. II./Grenadier-Regiment 499
E. I./Grenadier-Regiment 499
F. III./Grenadier-Regiment 499
G. Division Battalion 268
H. Division Reconnaissance
   elements
I. 268.Infanterie-Division
   command post
J. II./Grenadier-Regiment 480
   (Hauptman Hans Hemling)
K. III./Grenadier-Regiment 53
L. Kampfgruppe from 2.Panzer-
   Division

Note: gridlines are shown at intervals of 2km (1.25 miles)

39

A German patrol moves through an obstacle belt, September 1943. The German defensive lines typically included several lines of trenches and barbed-wire obstacles, which were effective in slowing infantry. However, once the Soviets learned how to coordinate their sappers and artillery, these types of positions could not stop the Red Army's advance. (Süddeutsche Zeitung Bild 00398363, Foto: Scherl)

over the German infantry strongpoints and I./Grenadier-Regiment 499 near Kamenka was overrun.

General der Infanterie Kurt von Tippelskirch, commander of XII Armeekorps, had very limited resources to plug any holes in his line, but he sent Greiner a single battalion – the III./Grenadier-Regiment 53 – which was itself on loan from Model's 9.Armee. During the rest of the afternoon, Trubnikov's infantry gradually began to outflank Linding's remaining strongpoints and once night fell, von Tippelskirch authorized Greiner to pull back 2–3km to form a new line. On the first day of the enemy offensive, XII Armeekorps had suffered over 600 casualties and lost its reinforced outpost lines, but the main positions of the Büffel-Stellung were still intact. In response, Heinrici directed a *Kampfgruppe* from 2.Panzer-Division, de-training east of Yelnya, to march to support 268.Infanterie-Division. Two other *Kampfgruppen*, one each from 36.Infanterie-Division and 56.Infanterie-Division, were sent by rail to Pavlinovo. However, the units arrived piecemeal and were committed as soon as they reached the area.

The only real Soviet success on the first day of *Suvorov* was achieved by General-mayor Vladimir A. Gluzdovsky's 31st Army against XXXIX Panzerkorps in the Yartsevo sector. The main effort was made by General-mayor Nikolai N. Oleshev's 36th Rifle Corps (215th, 274th and 359th Rifle divisions), with General-mayor Stanislav G. Poplavskiy's 45th Rifle Corps (220th and 331st Rifle divisions and the 42nd Guards Tank Brigade) in support. The two Soviet corps commanders leading this attack were an unusual lot; Oleshev was an NKVD officer, known for his ruthlessness in anti-partisan warfare, and Poplavskiy was a Polish communist. The 31st Army's attack started later than the main attacks and did not gather real steam until late in the day; Oleshev's 36th Rifle Corps attacked west of the Vop, a minor north–south river, while Poplavskiy's 45th Rifle Corps attacked east of the river. The Soviet attacks struck the inexperienced 113.Infanterie-Division, which had only been at the front for two weeks. Here, the Soviet artillery preparation succeeded in disrupting the defence because the inexperienced

German troops had not buried their communication wire deeply enough, so communication between the front-line units and the command elements was severed. Between 1800hrs and 2000hrs, Poplavskiy's 45th Rifle Corps overran a single German infantry battalion, II./Grenadier-Regiment 261, in the centre of the division's front and II./Grenadier-Regiment 260, which blocked a north–south road just east of the Vop. By 2100hrs, Soviet infantry managed to overrun a German artillery battery and it was clear that the 113.Infanterie-Division's front was breaking apart. During the night, both Grenadier-Regiment 260 and Grenadier-Regiment 261 fell back 2km, where the HKL was re-established behind the 6m-wide Vedosa River. Sensing confusion in the German ranks, Gluzdovsky committed his mobile group: Podpolkovnik Viktor F. Kotov's 42nd Guards Tank Brigade, which consisted of 50 tanks (seven KV-1, 21 T-34 and 22 T-60/70), a motorized rifle battalion, two motorcycle battalions and an anti-tank regiment with 20 76.2mm guns. Gluzdovsky ordered Kotov to push hard down the road east of the Vop to reach the Minsk–Moscow Highway, just 6km to the south. For a brief moment, it seemed that Poplavskiy's 45th Rifle Corps and Kotov's brigade might achieve a breakthrough.

Soviet sappers cutting German wire prior to an attack. Given that the wire is being cut in daylight, this obstacle is probably not under continuous observation. Indeed, this is likely a posed photo taken during training prior to the offensive. The 1st Sapper Brigade did play a major role in helping to breach German obstacles in the early stages of the offensive, but casualties were very heavy. (From Nik Cornish@ Stavka.org.uk)

Although German communications in this sector were disrupted, the commander of XXXIX Panzerkorps, General der Artillerie Robert Martinek, instinctively sent his reserves to Generalmajor Prüter's sector. A battery from Sturmgeschütz-Abteilung 185, the division Pionier battalion and a single infantry battalion, III./Grenadier-Regiment 260, arrived during the night and helped to stabilize the faltering 113.Infanterie-Division behind the Vedosa. During the day, 113.Infanterie-Division fired off 286 tons of artillery ammunition and 636,000 rounds of machine-gun ammunition, in a frantic effort to stop the Soviet attack. However, Heinrici would not yet allow 18.Panzergrenadier-Division to be committed to help XXXIX Panzerkorps, since he was worried about attacks elsewhere along his army's left flank. Although the Kalinin Front made only a minimal effort on the first day of *Suvorov*, Heinrici had to keep some kind of reserve in case Eremenko's front launched an all-out attack. Yet the German situation remained tenable because the Western Front's offensive was essentially a series of localized and uncoordinated attacks, rather than a simultaneous all-out effort to overwhelm 4.Armee on the ground and in the air. Thanks to the limited nature of *Suvorov*'s opening moves, 4.Armee was able to shuttle its limited reserves about to deal with one local crisis at a time.

During the first day of *Suvorov*, the Soviet 1st Air Army flew over 1,000 sorties, which was less than half what had been planned. Soviet histories suggest that overcast weather hindered their air operations, but German weather reports indicate the weather was perfect for flying on 7

113.INFANTERIE-DIVISION'S ORDEAL, 7–9 AUGUST 1943

Hitler ordered that the divisions lost at Stalingrad in February 1943 be immediately rebuilt with survivors and new recruits. The new 113.Infanterie-Division was hastily formed and sent to the Eastern Front, arriving just two weeks before Operation *Suvorov* began. On the first two days of the offensive, this inexperienced division nearly collapsed and 4.Armee was forced to commit its only reserves to prevent an enemy breakthrough in this sector.

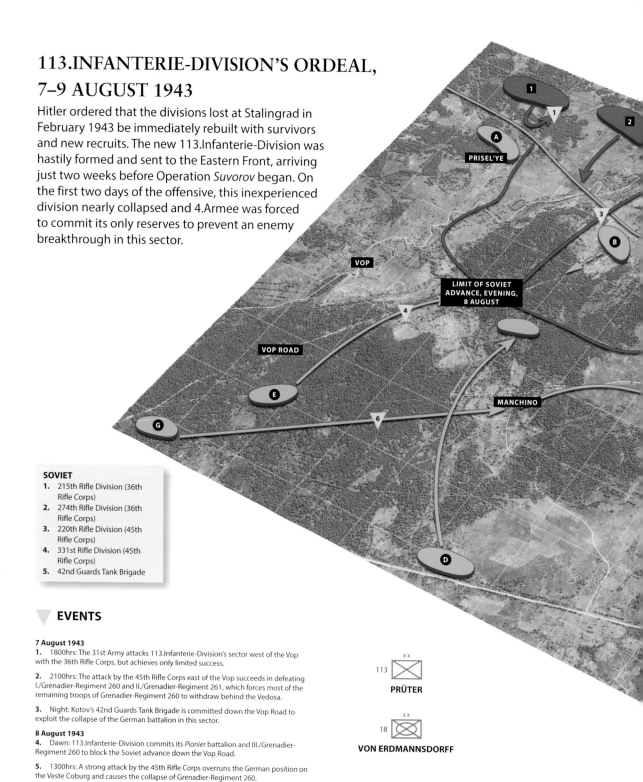

SOVIET
1. 215th Rifle Division (36th Rifle Corps)
2. 274th Rifle Division (36th Rifle Corps)
3. 220th Rifle Division (45th Rifle Corps)
4. 331st Rifle Division (45th Rifle Corps)
5. 42nd Guards Tank Brigade

EVENTS

7 August 1943
1. 1800hrs: The 31st Army attacks 113.Infanterie-Division's sector west of the Vop with the 36th Rifle Corps, but achieves only limited success.

2. 2100hrs: The attack by the 45th Rifle Corps east of the Vop succeeds in defeating I./Grenadier-Regiment 260 and II./Grenadier-Regiment 261, which forces most of the remaining troops of Grenadier-Regiment 260 to withdraw behind the Vedosa.

3. Night: Kotov's 42nd Guards Tank Brigade is committed down the Vop Road to exploit the collapse of the German battalion in this sector.

8 August 1943
4. Dawn: 113.Infanterie-Division commits its *Pionier* battalion and III./Grenadier-Regiment 260 to block the Soviet advance down the Vop Road.

5. 1300hrs: A strong attack by the 45th Rifle Corps overruns the German position on the Veste Coburg and causes the collapse of Grenadier-Regiment 260.

6. 1500hrs: The lead elements of 18.Panzergrenadier-Division arrive at Manchino to launch a counterattack, but are instead fed into the vacuum created by the collapse of Grenadier-Regiment 260.

7. 1800hrs: 18.Panzergrenadier-Division occupies positions south of the Vedosa to prevent a Soviet breakthrough.

9 August 1943
8. Morning: 18.Panzergrenadier-Division mounts a counterattack in a vain effort to re-establish the old front line north of the Vedosa, but it is repulsed with heavy losses.

113 ⊠ ˣˣ
PRÜTER

18 ⊠ ˣˣ
VON ERDMANNSDORFF

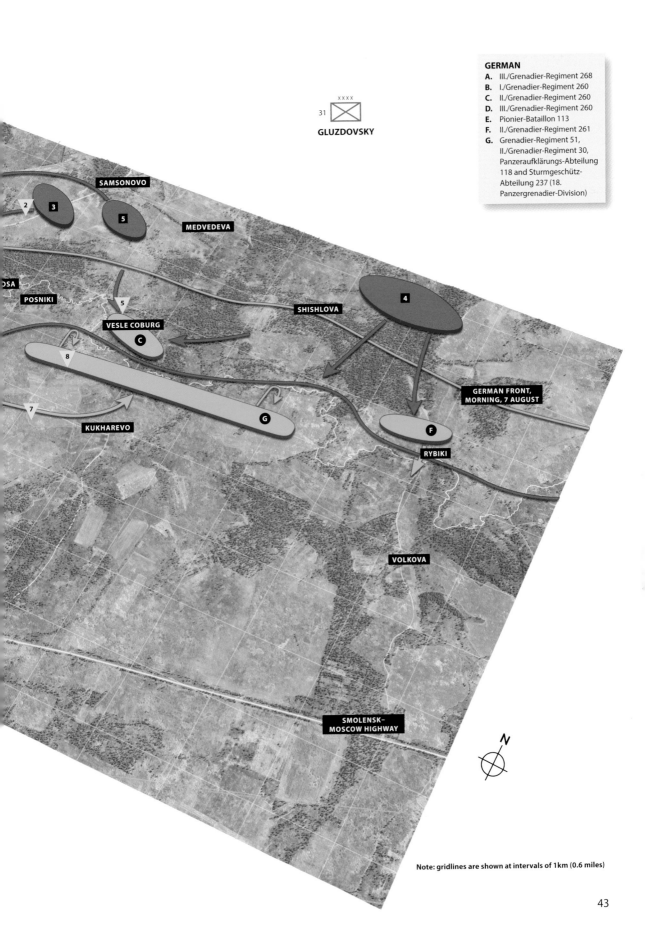

GLUZDOVSKY

xxxx
31

GERMAN
A. III./Grenadier-Regiment 268
B. I./Grenadier-Regiment 260
C. II./Grenadier-Regiment 260
D. III./Grenadier-Regiment 260
E. Pionier-Bataillon 113
F. II./Grenadier-Regiment 261
G. Grenadier-Regiment 51,
II./Grenadier-Regiment 30,
Panzeraufklärungs-Abteilung
118 and Sturmgeschütz-
Abteilung 237 (18.
Panzergrenadier-Division)

SAMSONOVO

MEDVEDEVA

POSNIKI

VESLE COBURG

SHISHLOVA

GERMAN FRONT,
MORNING, 7 AUGUST

KUKHAREVO

RYBIKI

VOLKOVA

SMOLENSK–
MOSCOW HIGHWAY

N

Note: gridlines are shown at intervals of 1km (0.6 miles)

A German *Pionier* NCO in a trench. Due to the shortage of infantrymen, German divisions were constantly forced to use their *Pioniere* to mount local counterattacks to restore lost positions. (From Nik Cornish@ Stavka.org.uk)

August. Indeed, the weather did not prevent von Greim's Luftflotte 6 from flying numerous Stuka and bomber sorties to attack Soviet concentrations. In addition, Jagdgeschwader 51 claimed 23 victories (ten fighters, eight Sturmoviks and five bombers) and 1st Air Army was unable to provide adequate air cover over the Western Front's shock groups. While Luftflotte 6 managed to inflict disproportionate losses on the enemy, the losses it did suffer were painful; Oberleutnant Heinrich Höfemeier, a 96-victory ace in Jagdgeschwader 51, was shot down by Soviet anti-aircraft fire and killed on the first day of *Suvorov*.

On the morning of 8 August, Sokolovsky resumed his offensive at 0730hrs, but now he had three armies tangled up on the main axis of advance. After a 30-minute artillery preparation, the Soviets resumed their attacks across a 10km-wide front, but the weight of the attack shifted to the left, against the village of Sluzna. The 164th Rifle Division and other elements of the 31st Army tried to take the village of Laski and thereby outflank the defenders in Sluzna, but were again stopped by Hauptman Hemling's stalwart II./Grenadier-Regiment 480; this was the beginning of a three-day battle for this small village. The 65th Guards Rifle Division continued its slow push towards Hill 233.3, with multiple infantry–tank assaults, but only succeeded in occupying the village of Veselukha after an advance of 1km. Trubnikov also committed his 22nd Guards Rifle Division from reserve, as well as the 1st Assault Engineer-Sapper Brigade, but efforts to penetrate the obstacle belts around Hill 233.3 failed. Amazingly, the best units in the 10th Guards Army were being held up by a battalion-sized outpost. Further west, Zhuralev's 68th Army inserted its 81st Rifle Corps (192nd Rifle Division, 199th Rifle Division) between the 10th Guards Army's two engaged corps, which put added pressure on Oberst Linding's battered Grenadier-Regiment 488. Von Tippelskirch sent three battalions of Grenadier-Regiment 118 (from 36.Infanterie-Division) forward to reinforce Greiner's sagging line, preventing a collapse. Nevertheless, both the 260. Infanterie-Division and 268.Infanterie-Division were being drained by steady losses and their front line was now held by a crazy patchwork of units from different divisions.

Elsewhere, Polenov's 5th Army continued its attack against IX Armeekorps in the Dorogobuzh sector, but only managed to advance 2–4km in the first 48 hours. Oberst von Eisenhart's Grenadier-Regiment 7 repelled multiple Soviet attacks, allegedly inflicting 3,000 dead upon Polenov's shock groups. Most of Polenov's tanks were knocked out by Panzerjägers, further reducing his remaining offensive capability. Further north, Gluzdovsky's 31st Army resumed its attack at dawn and gained some more ground against 113.Infanterie-Division, whose troops were near collapse. By early afternoon, Grenadier-Regiment 260 cracked after losing a key defensive position known as the 'Veste Coburg' (Hill 216.6) and the Soviet 220th Rifle Division surged into the gap, just east of the Vop. Heinrici decided to give Martinek his only real reserve, Generalleutnant Werner von Erdmannsdorff's

18.Panzergrenadier-Division, and he ordered XXXIX Panzerkorps to mount an immediate counterattack. The 4.Armee also requested Luftflotte 6 to prioritize air support to this sector. Around 1500hrs, Martinek commenced his counterattack with Grenadier-Regiment 51, II./Grenadier-Regiment 30, Panzeraufklärungs-Abteilung 118 and Sturmgeschütz-Abteilung 237. Just as the counterattack force approached the village of Manchino, they encountered fleeing German troops from the shattered I./Grenadier-Regiment 260. One German officer was shocked to see these demoralized troops – some half-naked and most without weapons – retreating in disorganized panic. Efforts to halt their retreat failed. The counterattack force pressed onwards and managed to check any further Soviet advance, while also re-establishing contact with isolated elements from another German battalion (II./Grenadier-Regiment 261). The Luftwaffe provided substantial assistance, by mounting over 100 close air support sorties that bombed and strafed movement along the Vop road. Fighters from Jagdgeschwader 51 also helped to disrupt Soviet air support and on 8 August the Jagdgruppe claimed 26 victories (eight fighters and 18 Sturmoviks).

On 9 August, Gluzdovsky's 31st Army continued to try and batter its way through the left flank of 113.Infanterie-Division, but could not make any further progress due to the presence of 18.Panzergrenadier-Division and its assault guns. Kotov's 42nd Guards Tank Brigade failed to reach the Minsk–Moscow Highway and lost 35 of its tanks and 176 troops. The 18.Panzergrenadier-Division conducted a major counterattack in a vain effort to restore the original front line, but suffered heavy losses due to strong Soviet artillery fire and the inability of its assault guns to get across the Vedosa. Von Kluge was furious with Martinek for the bungled nature of the counterattack and the misuse of his sole mobile reserve. However, 113.Infanterie-Division had suffered more than 1,700 casualties during the first three days of the campaign and could only maintain its HKL by committing its Field Replacement Battalion, reconnaissance and *Pionier* battalions into the line as infantry. Nor could 18.Panzergrenadier-Division be released, since it was now needed to hold a substantial section of the front. Thus, Gluzdovsky had failed to achieve a breakthrough, but he had succeeded in fixing the German reserves.

Gordov's 33rd Army continued attacking on 9–10 August with three rifle divisions on a very narrow front and finally managed to push Hemling's II./Grenadier-Regiment 480 out of most of Sluzna, but was then stymied around the villages of Laski and Gubino. The 260.Infanterie-Division was forced to commit an ad hoc battalion under Hauptman Felix Osterman, which narrowly prevented a Soviet breakthrough. Trubnikov's 10th Guards Army almost clawed its way onto Hill 233.3 on 9 August, but was thrown back by a furious German counterattack. The hilltop was held by Major Kurt Brill's I./Grenadier-Regiment 488, a company of *Pioniere* and some assault guns. A *Kampfgruppe* from 2.Panzer-Division (a company of tanks and part of the armoured reconnaissance battalion) arrived and managed to temporarily stabilize the situation on the left flank of Greiner's 268.Infanterie Division. By this point, Trubnikov had become fixated on Hill 233.3 and failed to see that the German flanks were vulnerable. Instead, he settled into a slugging match for the hill, which allowed the Germans to economize on their limited reserves. After three days of combat, XII Armeekorps was seriously stressed by casualties and was forced to start abandoning some of

THE CAPTURE OF HILL 233.3, 2100HRS, 10 AUGUST 1943 (PP. 46–47)

In the opening phase of Operation *Suvorov*, the Western Front made its main effort in the centre, intending to break through to the Smolensk–Spas-Demensk railway line on the first day of the offensive, then pivot north-west to seize Yelnya. However, Sokolovsky had not taken into account the fierce resistance of the German XII Armeekorps in the Büffel-Stellung, particularly the critical position of Hill 233.3 near the village of Gnezdilovo. Soviet reconnaissance failed to note the strength of this position prior to the offensive, so it came as a surprise when Trubnikov's 10th Guards Army shock groups were fought to a standstill on the first day of the offensive. The heavily defended hilltop was held by Major Kurt Brill's I./Grenadier-Regiment 488, a company of *Pioniere*, Panzerjägers and assault guns. Trubnikov's troops attacked the German positions on Hill 233.3 for four days but were repeatedly thrown back with heavy losses. It was only when the German flanking positions began to crumble that XII Armeekorps lost its grip on this critical position. On the afternoon of 10 August, Trubnikov committed all his remaining infantry, tanks and sappers to seize Hill 233.3, which was blasted for 50 minutes by Soviet heavy artillery. After six hours of fighting,

troops from the 29th Guards Rifle Division and 23rd Tank Brigade finally reached the summit, but still needed another hour to mop up the German rear-guards. Only nine German soldiers were captured atop Hill 233.3.

In this scene, Soviet infantrymen (**1**) from the 29th Guards Rifle Division and T-34 tanks (**2**) from the 23rd Tank Brigade are approaching the devastated crest of Hill 233.3. The village of Veselukha (**3**) lies burning in the background. Most of Brill's battalion withdrew before the end, leaving a small rear-guard to delay Trubnikov's troops for as long as possible. A 5cm Pak 38 anti-tank gun (**4**) and MG34 heavy machine gun (**5**) position have finally been silenced. The slope of Hill 233.3 is carpeted with Soviet casualties and knocked-out T-34 tanks. Although the German defence of Hill 233.3 seriously unhinged Sokolovsky's operational schedule and inflicted crippling losses on Trubnikov's assault divisions, it ultimately failed to stop the 10th Guards Army from reaching the railway line. After losing the Büffel-Stellung, XII Armeekorps was forced to trade space for time until Sokolovsky's offensive outran its logistical support.

A camouflaged German bunker in a wooded area. The trick was to prevent the enemy from learning the location of bunkers in the main line of resistance (HKL) prior to the battle, so that these unidentified positions could survive the artillery bombardment and inflict maximum casualties on the first wave of assault infantry. It was particularly difficult to identify bunkers in the thickly wooded areas where Operation *Suvorov* took place. (From Nik Cornish@ Stavka.org.uk)

its more exposed positions before they were enveloped. Nevertheless, Brill's battalion continued to resist tenaciously on Hill 233.3 until overwhelmed by a massive Soviet attack on the evening of 10 August. Trubnikov still had one ace up his sleeve – General-mayor Andrei T. Stuchenko's 29th Guards Rifle Division – which had been kept in reserve for the first day of the operation. Stuchenko had miraculously escaped from the Vyazma pocket in October 1941, where his first division was destroyed, and was a veteran commander. Stuchenko's division, along with attached tanks and sappers, assaulted the hilltop after a 50-minute artillery barrage and finally secured this position by 2200hrs.

On 10 August, Sokolovsky ordered General-leytenant Vasiliy S. Popov's 10th Army to attack north-west out of the Kirov salient, against LVI Panzerkorps. Apparently Heinrici was not expecting an attack from this direction, because three Soviet rifle divisions (the 247th, 290th and 330th) were able to punch through the left flank of 321.Infanterie-Division and advanced 5km on the first day. By nightfall, Popov's under-resourced 10th Army – which had very modest artillery and tank support – was the only one of Sokolovsky's armies to have achieved a breakthrough. Heinrici tried to rush 9.Panzer-Division, which was in transit, to this sector but it was clear that the damage was done when Popov began to roll up the neighbouring 131.Infanterie-Division. Grudgingly, the right flank of 4.Armee began to give up some ground and fall back to secondary positions. Yet since Popov had not been provided resources to form a mobile group, he did not have the means at hand to exploit his success. Sokolovsky decided to transfer both Volkov's 5th Mechanized Corps and Sokolov's 6th Guards Cavalry Corps from Trubnikov's stalled 10th Guards Army to Popov's command, although this involved moving a distance of more than 70km at night. Neither corps would be in a position to attack before 12 August at the earliest.

By 11 August, Sturmgeschütz-Abteilung 667 only had four of its original 20 assault guns still operational and almost all vehicle commanders were casualties, but the unit had knocked out 31 enemy tanks. Altogether, XII Armeekorps claimed 72 enemy tanks knocked out, including ten in close combat. Yet despite the arrival of three infantry battalions (Grenadier-Regiment 87) from 36.Infanterie-Division, it was clear that XII Armeekorps was running out of infantry and could no longer hold the Büffel-Stellung, so late on 11 August, the Germans began falling back toward the Yelnya–Spas-Demensk railway. Although Sokolovsky's plan for the first phase of *Suvorov* had not gone according to schedule, the offensive seemed to be on the verge of accomplishing its initial objectives. Unfortunately, Sokolovsky's artillery had expended virtually all of its ammunition and the 1st Air Army was unable to provide adequate air support. With both the 5th Mechanized Corps and 6th Guards Cavalry Corps in transit, Sokolovsky was not able to immediately exploit the German withdrawal. The Soviet offensive was in an awkward position. Furthermore, Oberst Johannes Jollasse arrived with 9.Panzer-Division and helped to seal off Popov's breakthrough before LVI Panzerkorps' front entirely collapsed. Despite suffering heavy losses during *Zitadelle*, 9.Panzer-Division still had 36 operational tanks, 218 half-tracks and armoured cars and a battalion of the new Wespe self-propelled artillery pieces. Local counterattacks quickly halted Popov's infantry.

On 12 August, Trubnikov's 10th Guards Army made another major push and captured the village of Gnezdilovo. Reinforcements continued to trickle in from Model's 9.Armee; Grenadier-Regiment 482 from 262.Infanterie-Division arrived and was immediately thrust into the path of Trubnikov's shock groups, but was quickly overwhelmed by 1100hrs. By late afternoon, XII Armeekorps' front north of the railway was crumbling and Trubnikov's infantry and tanks were leaking through the gaps in the German defence. By the end of the day, the lead elements of the 10th Guards Army were approaching Pavlinovo and some Soviet troops had already reached the rail line. If Sokolovsky had not transferred Volkov's 5th Mechanized Corps to Popov's 10th Army, Trubnikov might have been able to exploit the sudden German collapse in the XII Armeekorps sector. However, Trubnikov's armour was seriously depleted by this point and he had no mobile group to harry the retreating Germans.

Given the collapse in the XII Armeekorps sector and the imminent enemy attack with the 5th Mechanized Corps from the south-east, Heinrici had no choice but to order XII Armeekorps to evacuate the town of Spas-

German infantry observe enemy movement to their front from the edge of a wood line. The range of tactical engagements was often far shorter in the heavily wooded terrain east of Smolensk, with most actions occurring within a few hundred metres. (From Nik Cornish@ Stavka.org.uk)

Demensk on the night of 12/13 August. German support troops evacuated in haste and left several supply depots intact. On the morning of 13 August, 146th Rifle Division of 49th Army was the first unit to enter Spas-Demensk, followed by 42nd Rifle Division and 256th Tank Brigade from 33rd Army. The town itself was deserted. Spas-Demensk had a pre-war population of 4,200, but by this point in the war most civilians had either been removed by the Germans or run off into the woods. Both the 49th and 33rd armies continued advancing into the void south-west of

The Germans continued to take significant numbers of enemy prisoners during the early stages of *Suvorov*, when Soviet casualties were very heavy. However, once the Germans began to retreat, fewer prisoners were taken. Many Soviet prisoners volunteered to serve with the Wehrmacht as auxiliaries (known to the Germans as 'Hiwis') rather than go to POW camps. After liberation, most former Soviet POWs were sent to the Gulag so the NKVD could determine who had collaborated with the enemy. (Author's collection)

Spas-Demensk. Having encountered numerous difficulties in shifting to the Kirov sector, Volkov's 5th Mechanized Corps was sent into liberated Spas-Demensk with the intent of pushing west into XII Armeekorps' crumbling right flank. Unfortunately, Volkhov's movement was spotted by Luftwaffe reconnaissance and von Greim ordered a massive aerial attack on the concentrated enemy mechanized force. A raid by 60 German bombers caught 5th Mechanized Corps packed in the streets of Spas-Demensk and destroyed a significant number of tanks and vehicles. Over the next three days, Luftflotte 6 conducted five more major attacks on Volkhov's corps, which was battered into combat ineffectiveness before it could strike a major blow. The Soviets were quick to blame the decimation of 5th Mechanized Corps on the alleged poor quality of its Lend-Lease tanks, rather than the failure of Gromov's 1st Air Army to provide effective air cover. The 5th Mechanized Corps was eventually used to conduct a minor attack south of Spas-Demensk, against 9.Panzer-Division's positions along the Bolva River. Although the attack succeeded in convincing the Germans to withdraw further, Leytenant Dmitry F. Loza, who commanded a company of Matilda tanks in 233rd Tank Brigade observed a fratricide incident. Soviet anti-tank gunners fired upon one company, assuming the Lend-Lease tanks were German vehicles. Three Matildas were accidently destroyed, which added further injury to 5th Mechanized Corps' inauspicious entry into battle.

Meanwhile, Sokolov's 6th Guards Cavalry Corps was committed east of Pavlinovo into the 33rd Army sector on the night of 12/13 August. Sokolov's corps had been ordered hither and yon for 72 hours, exhausting and disordering its units, before it was hastily committed again to battle on the morning of 13 August. Von Tippelskirch's XII Armeekorps was forced to abandon Pavlinovo and conduct a delaying operation. Although hard-pressed, XII Armeekorps was able to establish a new front line 5km south of Pavlinovo during the night. By the time that Sokolov's cavalrymen attacked on the morning of 13 August, the Germans were no longer retreating but defending. Sokolov's 6th Guards Cavalry Corps was repulsed with significant loss, meaning that Trubnikov no longer had enough remaining combat power to effect a true breakthrough.

At 0730hrs on 13 August, Eremenko's Kalinin Front finally joined the offensive, by attacking General der Infanterie Paul Völckers' XXVII Armeekorps 8km north-east of Dukhovshchina. The main effort was made on the Kalinin Front's left flank by General-leytenant Aleksei I. Zygin's 39th Army, with five rifle divisions from 2nd Guards Rifle Corps and 83rd Rifle Corps, supported by two tank brigades, two tank regiments and two sapper brigades. General-leytenant Konstantin D. Golubev's 43rd Army conducted a supporting attack on the right with two rifle divisions and a tank regiment. Papivin's 3rd Air Army provided air cover. Völckers had three infantry divisions (52., 197. and 256.Infanterie) defending a 40km-wide front and another infantry division (246.Infanterie) in reserve behind the front. All four of these divisions possessed only six instead of nine infantry battalions and most of these battalions were at 45–50 per cent of authorized strength. The corps reserve consisted of a single *Pionier* battalion. Although Völckers' infantry units were thinly spread, the Barbarossa-Stellung was a well-constructed position consisting of three successive lines of trenches in heavily wooded terrain, sitting atop high ground.

Eremenko only had enough ammunition for a 35-minute artillery preparation, which failed to suppress the German defences. In the first few hours, General-leytenant Afanasy P. Beloborodov's 2nd Guards Rifle Corps from 39th Army managed to penetrate the first trench line of 52.Infanterie-Division south-east of Spas-Ugly and overrun one German battalion. However, Zygin's shock groups were only able to advance 1,500m before being stopped by German counterattacks (not the 2–4km claimed by the author Vasily Istomin). Division-level Panzerjägers, equipped with the potent 7.5cm Pak 40 anti-tank guns, knocked out 45 enemy tanks in the first two days. Also on the 13th, Golubev's 43rd Army conducted a supporting attack against 197.Infanterie-Division, which succeeded in capturing a pair of front-line villages. In response to Eremenko's offensive, Völckers decided to break up 246.Infanterie-Division and use its components to reinforce the weakened 52.Infanterie-Division.

On the afternoon of 14 August, von Greim arrived at Völckers' corps command post to personally coordinate Luftwaffe strikes against 39th Army's penetration. After this, Luftwaffe air attacks intensified and seriously disrupted Zygin's formations. Just as 52.Infanterie-Division was forced to abandon more positions, the first German reinforcements began to arrive: schwere Panzerjäger-Abteilung 655 (equipped with 14 of the new Hornisse tank destroyers), I./Flak-Lehr-Regiment (gem. mot.), which had a mix of 2cm and 8.8cm Flak guns, and Nebelwerfer-Regiment 51 (including two batteries with the new Panzerwerfer 42, a 15cm multiple rocket launcher mounted on an armoured Maultier half-track). The additional firepower enabled Völckers to mount a series of powerful local counterattacks, which brought a brief respite from Zygin's attacks. However, Völckers was desperately short of infantry and it was only the arrival of the lead elements of 25.Panzergrenadier-Division that enabled him to stabilize his front line. The Panzerarmee 3, which was not under attack, was also able to contribute a few infantry battalions and some assault guns. In four days of heavy fighting, Zygin's troops only managed to advance about 3km and failed to reach any of their objectives. Russian post-war histories are particularly silent about the Kalinin Front offensive in August 1943. Yet the XXVII Armeekorps had suffered over 3,000 casualties – including about one-third of its infantrymen

A sniper unit in the Kalinin Front receives instruction on tactics. Note the camouflage net covers worn on the M40 helmets – this was extremely rare. The mix of different sniper weapons – both the Mosin–Nagant 1891/30 and the SVT-40 – should also be noted. One of the primary tasks of these snipers was to eliminate German machine gunners, which could seriously reduce enemy defensive firepower during an assault. (Author's collection)

– and 25.Panzergrenadier-Division was now obliged to take over a section of the front.

By 14 August, the fighting was beginning to ebb in the other sectors due to heavy combat losses, fatigue and shortage of artillery ammunition. Sokolovsky committed General-leytenant Nikolai I. Krylov's 21st Army into Trubnikov's sector in order to allow the 10th Guards Army to reconstitute itself. Krylov's army had almost no support units and it quickly suffered disproportionate losses. A final surge by the 21st, 33rd and 49th armies on 14–15 August failed to budge XII Armeekorps, which, in one of those stunning demonstrations of the Wehrmacht's improvisational skill, had somehow managed to establish a new continuous front. The 1st Air Army committed its ground attack units en masse to support a breakthrough but suffered crippling losses from Jagdgeschwader 51's fighters. Martinek's XXXIX Panzerkorps and Schmidt's IX Armeekorps also managed to stabilize their sectors, without losing any additional terrain. It was apparent that the Western Front was rapidly approaching the culmination point (in military terminology, the point where the offense is no longer stronger than the defence). The weather also took a turn for the worse, with a rainy period setting in during 15–20 August, which limited air operations by both sides. However, the deciding factor on whether to continue *Suvorov* was determined by Soviet supply shortages, which were approaching a catastrophic state; all units were short of artillery ammunition, the 1st Air Army was short of fuel and some rifle units reported that they were running out of rifle ammunition. The offensive had not been provisioned for a protracted battle and now the stocks were virtually exhausted. The 4.Armee was also running short on artillery ammunition, particularly in the XII Armeekorps sector, but still had enough to continue the battle. Although Stavka was reluctant to suspend *Suvorov*, on 21 August Sokolovsky was finally authorized to temporarily suspend offensive operations until he could replenish his assault units. He was given one week.

German losses during the initial phase of Operation *Suvorov* were heavy and few replacements were arriving. Heinrici took several risky measures to try and create small local reserves. He ordered his army-level training staff to cannibalize its weapons school and use its cadre to create an ad hoc unit known as Armee-Sturm Regiment AOK 4; this gave Heinrici a spare infantry regiment but it also meant that he no longer had veteran instructors to train any further replacements. In addition, he combined the remnants of 56.Infanterie-Division and 262.Infanterie-Division (also sent from 9.Armee) into Kampfgruppe Vincenz, which enabled the *Kampfgruppe* from 2.Panzer-Division to pull out of the line east of Yelnya and begin refitting. However, Kampfgruppe Vincenz was left to defend the direct route to Yelnya with barely 1,000 infantrymen in five threadbare battalions. Heinrici transferred the badly depleted 18.Panzer-Division to backstop Völckers' XXVII Armeekorps and protect his left flank, although this unit had just 1,200 infantrymen and 13 tanks. Furthermore, once it was clear that the Western Front had suspended its offensive, Model wasted no time in demanding that the units he transferred to 4.Armee be returned at once. Model's own 9.Armee had just retreated into the Hagen Stellung and was still under heavy attack; if this position was lost, Heinrici's right flank would be at risk. Consequently, von Kluge was forced to make hard choices about allocating his almost negligible reserves. Von Kluge managed to keep the half-strength 330.Infanterie-Division as an army group reserve, but he had no mobile reserves left.

Overall, 4.Armee suffered 28,000 casualties between 1 and 20 August, including 7,239 dead or missing. The XII Armeekorps was the hardest hit, having suffered over 5,000 casualties and 268.Infanterie-Division was reduced to a battlegroup. Material losses in XII Armeekorps were also heavy – 67 artillery pieces, 206 anti-tank guns, 158 medium mortars and 1,482 machine guns – which greatly reduced the defensive firepower of the remaining troops. In XXXIX Panzerkorps, 113.Infanterie-Division suffered 1,738 casualties and 18.Panzergrenadier-Division suffered 1,526 casualties. In Völckers' XXVII Armeekorps, 52.Infanterie-Division lost 60 per cent of its infantry, 30 per cent of its artillery and 84 per cent of its anti-tank guns in a week of fighting; its infantry battalions were left with an average of 169 troops – less than one full-strength company. Heinrici's 4.Armee had survived the first phase of *Suvorov*, but many of its front-line infantry battalions were now reduced to less than one-third of their authorized strength and Heeresgruppe Mitte had no further reserves to provide.

A destroyed T-34/76 medium tank. The Western Front used its armour in company-size groups to support infantry attacks, but suffered heavy losses in the initial phase of the operation from the improved generation of German anti-tank guns, such as the 7.5cm Pak 40. (From Nik Cornish@ Stavka.org.uk)

In the air, Luftflotte 6 dominated the numerically superior 1st Air Army and 3rd Air Army, inflicting disproportionate losses; the Soviet air armies involved in the first phase of *Suvorov* lost about 300 aircraft to enemy action, compared to about 50 for Greim's formations. In particular, the Il-2 ground-attack units were repeatedly intercepted by Jagdgeschwader 51's Fw-190 fighters and ripped apart; 1st Air Army lost about 40 per cent of its Il-2s in the first two weeks. In air-to-air combat, the Fw-190 demonstrated clear superiority over the La-5 and prevented Gromov from achieving air superiority over the battlefield. Indeed, the Luftwaffe played a major role in wearing down the Soviet attackers.

Soviet losses during the first phase of *Suvorov* were even heavier. Trubnikov's 10th Guards Army had suffered 30 per cent casualties and its best unit, the 65th Guards Rifle Division, had been decimated, having lost 75 per cent of its personnel killed or wounded in just seven days of fighting. Altogether, the Western Front suffered roughly 75,000 casualties in the first phase

A German StuG III assault gun on a road in September 1943. The assault gun units in Heeresgruppe Mitte still possessed a number of the older Ausf. C, D and E models, equipped with the short-barrelled 7.5cm L/24 gun. The assault guns were usually employed as individual batteries of six to eight vehicles to support an infantry division. (Bundesarchiv, Bild 101I-154-1986-04, Foto: Ludwig Knobloch)

of *Suvorov*, including about 20,000 dead or missing. The Kalinin Front's losses are more obscure, but probably at least 10,000 casualties. In other words, 4.Armee inflicted roughly 3:1 casualties upon the Western and Kalinin fronts. During the first phase of *Suvorov*, the Western Front received only limited reinforcements to replace its losses and just enough supplies to keep the offensive sputtering along. In order to restock his shattered armoured units, Sokolovsky received 196th Tank Brigade and 43rd Guards Tank Brigade from the RVGK. However, these two brigades only possessed a total of 78 tanks, only ten of which were T-34s; most of the rest were a mix of Matildas, Valentines, Grants and Stuart tanks. Eventually, on 20 August, Sokolovsky received General-mayor Alexei S. Burdeyney's 2nd Guards Tank Corps (formerly the 24th Tank Corps), which was rebuilt after the Tatsinskaya Raid in December 1942 and recently fought at Kursk. Burdeyney's 2nd Guards Tank Corps had 201 tanks, including 131 T-34s.

THE SECOND ROUND, 23 AUGUST–7 SEPTEMBER 1943

Stavka granted Sokolovsky only one week to reorganize for the next push. The Western Front staff hastily drafted a revised offensive plan – approved on 22 August – which placed the main effort in the centre, with the 10th Guards Army and the 21st, 33rd and 68th armies. These forces would attack XII Armeekorps all along its front until it shattered, then push mobile groups through the gaps to seize Yelnya. Simultaneously, the 5th and 31st armies would conduct a supporting operation to pierce the front of IX Armeekorps and XXXIX Panzerkorps in order to seize the cities of Dorogobuzh and Yartsevo. Virtually all of the units on both sides were well below authorized strength, making the second phase of *Suvorov* a contest to see which side could outlast the other.

As Stavka representative, Marshal Voronov worked to get more artillery ammunition allocated to the Western Front and he helped reorganize the

artillery. Krylov's 21st Army was reinforced with seven artillery brigades and a sapper brigade, plus given the 2nd Guards Tank Corps as an exploitation force. Gordov's 33rd Army was provided five artillery brigades, as well as the 5th Mechanized Corps and 6th Guards Cavalry Corps. This time, Sokolovsky intended to commit his primary manoeuvre units together, along the same axis, once the enemy front-line defences were overcome. The shortage of artillery ammunition and fuel was persistent, due to the competing needs of other fronts, but enough was gathered for another short offensive pulse. The Western Front directed the 5th and 10th armies to conduct intensive *maskirovka* operations in their sectors between 23 and 27 August in order to deceive the Germans about where the blow would fall. Obsolete light tanks like the T-60 were used to simulate large-scale tank movements just behind the front, while the enemy was also allowed to see the transfer of artillery units to these sectors. It is unknown if the Soviet *maskirovka* operations had any effect, but it was not difficult for Heinrici to see where Sokolovsky would attack next.

Gromov's 1st Air Army used the brief respite to rotate some of its regiments in order to use rested units for the next phase of the offensive. The French Normandie-Niemen Group, equipped with Yak-1M fighters, moved into the recently cleared Spas-Demensk airfield on 24 August. Papivin's 3rd Air Army was significantly reinforced by the addition of another fighter division (240th Fighter Aviation Division), three Sturmovik regiments and two Pe-2 regiments.

The Red Army also used the inter-regnum to settle scores in liberated territory. People who had collaborated with the Germans were identified and dealt with by summary justice. In the village of Osinovka, a village elder who had cooperated with the Germans was hanged and a sign was affixed to his corpse that read, 'For betrayal of the Motherland – Death!' Now that the Red Army was advancing westwards, its leadership was intent that whoever had consorted with the occupation should be rooted out and eliminated.

There was little Heinrici could do to stiffen his defences during the brief respite. Von Tippelskirch's XII Armeekorps was no longer occupying prepared positions and it had barely enough troops to hold a continuous front. Army-level construction units such as Baupionier-Bataillon 46

Second phase of Operation *Suvorov*, 28 August 1943

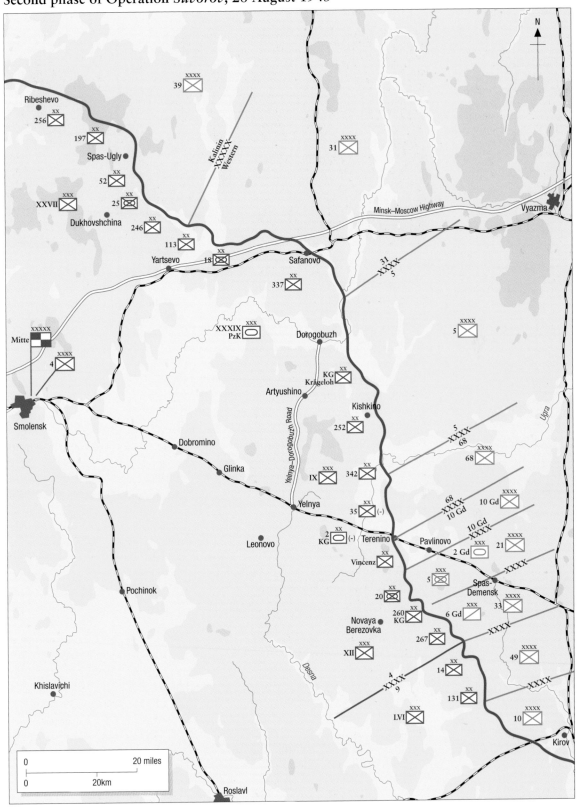

A Soviet 152mm howitzer M1910/37 howitzer in action. Although obsolescent by 1943, older weapons like this were still used by the artillery regiments in Soviet rifle divisions, while newer guns went to the corps- and front-level artillery units. This weapon had shorter range than German division-level artillery pieces and was not particularly easy to move about the battlefield. (From Nik Cornish@ Stavka.org.uk)

attempted to create new field works in the short time available, but only succeeded in creating a thin line of trenches, but no bunkers. Yelnya was a major supply depot but it was only defended by a Flak battalion and security troops from Korück 559. In an effort to reinforce the thin line east of Yelnya, on 21 August Heinrici transferred the bulk of 35.Infanterie-Division from XXXIX Panzerkorps sector and sent it south to reinforce the left flank of XII Armeekorps, leaving only Gruppe Krägeloh (a reinforced Grenadier-Regiment 111) to hold a division-sized sector south of Dorogobuzh. The 337. Infanterie-Division north of Dorogobuzh was obliged to hold a sector that was 25km wide – nearly triple the normal defensive sector. Given the tenuous nature of 4.Armee's front, the only logical solution was for Heeresgruppe Mitte to retire behind a major natural obstacle, such as either the Desna River or the Dnepr River. On 12 August, Hitler had authorized the Panther-Stellung, intended to be a major line of fortifications stretching from the Baltic to the Black Sea. However, impressive-sounding projects such as the Panther-Stellung cannot be conjured out of thin air and construction was not even scheduled to begin until early September. Hitler ordered von Kluge to hold his current positions until the Panther-Stellung was ready, which meant for at least another 4–6 weeks. Consequently, Heinrici was expected to hold his thinly manned front for an extended period without hope of further reinforcements – a recipe for disaster.

A Hornisse tank destroyer in action. In early September 1943, 4.Armee received schwere Panzerjäger-Abteilung 655, equipped with the new Hornisse tank destroyer. Armed with the same long-barrelled 8.8cm gun as the towed Pak 43, the Hornisse was a formidable anti-tank weapon. When over-watching open terrain like this, the Hornisse could destroy T-34 tanks out to 2,000m or more, beyond the effective range of Soviet tank guns. (Bundesarchiv, Bild 101I-278-0860-13, Foto: Jacob)

A German 2cm light Flak gun, mounted on an SdKfz 10 half-track, in action in a wooded area. The Germans habitually used their self-propelled light Flak guns in the direct-fire role because they were well suited for engaging enemy infantry at long range. (From Nik Cornish@ Stavka.org.uk)

Having started his offensive later than the Western Front, Eremenko was in a better position to resume operations after a shorter break. Reinforced by the 5th Guards Rifle Corps from the 3rd Shock Army at Velikiye Luki, Zygin's 39th Army attacked XXVII Armeekorps on 25 August, in exactly the same sector where it had previously attacked. The 5th Guards Rifle Corps managed to create a minor bulge in the German front, 1km deep and 3km wide, but otherwise little was achieved in five days of fighting. The 25.Panzergrenadier-Division anchored the German defence in the Barbarossa-Stellung and Eremenko's shortage of ammunition and fuel made it difficult for him to commit more than a few divisions at a time. The Kalinin Front was stymied. Eremenko sent a request to Stavka for more artillery ammunition and 12 days to replenish his combat units. In his memoirs, Eremenko wrote:

> I was seriously worried that the offensive was fading, and the task was not completed, although we did not lack people. The main cause of our failure was the inability of the artillery to destroy the enemy's strongly fortified positions. The essence of the matter was not in the number of barrels of artillery, but in the number of shells. In terms of ammunition, we were kept on a starvation ration and yet at the same time, ordered to make rapid progress. In connection with the situation on other sectors of the front, Stavka did not have the ability to provide us with sufficient ammunition.

Stalin was unmoved by Eremenko's requests and ordered him to continue attacking.

Sokolovsky planned to resume the offensive on 28 August, during a period of clear weather. Just prior to the resumption of the Soviet offensive, von Kluge decided to tinker with front-line command arrangements because Model was constantly complaining about transferring so many formations to Heinrici's 4.Armee. Now, von Kluge transferred XII Armeekorps to 9.Armee, where it was merged with LVI Panzerkorps and, together, the new formation

THE WITHDRAWAL FROM YELNYA, 30 AUGUST 1943 (PP. 60–61)

Within three days of the resumption of the Soviet Western Front offensive, the German XII Armeekorps front was broken and Soviet armour and infantry advanced rapidly towards Yelnya. Since late 1941, the Germans had developed Yelnya into a major forward supply base to support 4.Armee and it stored stockpiles of food, ammunition and fuel. However, 4.Armee had no reserves immediately available to block the Soviet advance and instead XII Armeekorps was ordered to evacuate the city. Any material that could not be moved in the short time available was to be destroyed. An ad hoc unit dubbed Kampfgruppe Beyse under the command of a reserve artillery officer conducted the rear-guard action in Yelnya on the afternoon of 30 August. Beyse and his troops were terrified of being captured by the on-rushing Soviet tanks and infantry, so they worked frantically to do as much damage as possible in a few hours. In fact, most of the supply depots were abandoned intact and had to be bombed later by the Luftwaffe.

In this scene, German *Pioniere* and rear-area troops from Kampfgruppe Beyse are conducting hasty demolitions along a railway line on the western outskirts of Yelnya. While a German officer (**1**) shouts orders to hurry, two *Pionier Feldwebel* (**2**) are setting an explosive charge under a railway culvert. Other troops are running along the track, having set other charges. In the background, civilian housing in Yelnya burns, set alight by the retreating Germans. The scene is one of chaos and confusion, which would be repeated in one Russian town after another as the defeated Wehrmacht fell back towards the Reich. Most of the able-bodied civilians were also evacuated and farm animals that could not be moved in time were gunned down. Hitler demanded that retreating German units conduct ruthless 'scorched-earth' tactics to deny resources to the enemy and hinder their advance. However, German scorched-earth tactics also encouraged Soviet troops to be equally destructive with civilian property when they reached German territory in 1944.

was designated Gruppe Harpe. All of the units from XII Armeekorps defending the eastern approaches to Yelnya were transferred to Schmidt's IX Armeekorps, which was now responsible for defending a 50km-wide sector from south of Dorogobuzh to the town of Novaya Berezovka, south-east of Yelnya. Last-minute command alterations of this sort tend to cause more chaos than they are worth and the German defence was already weak and disorganized. Von Kluge also placed the *Kampfgruppe* from 2.Panzer-Division (which was resting along the railway line east of Yelnya) under his control, rather than Heinrici's, which induced further delay into the commitment of the only significant reserve in the Yelnya sector.

At 0800hrs on 28 August, the Western Front began a 90-minute artillery preparation across a 25km-wide front south-east of Yelnya, in the sectors of the 10th Guards, 21st and 33rd armies. The ADD fired counter-battery missions against the German divisional artillery positions while multiple rocket launchers pounded the front-line infantry positions, suppressing some of them. Around 0930hrs, the artillery fire lifted and Soviet infantry and tanks began to advance westwards. However, instead of choosing the obvious axis of advance straight up the railway line towards Yelnya, Sokolovsky decided to make his main effort in the 33rd Army sector against the boundary between Schmidt's IX Armeekorps and Gruppe Harpe, near Novaya Berezovka. The 20.Panzergrenadier-Division was squarely in the path of Gordov's 33rd Army and it was pushed back on its heels, away from its linkage with the right flank of IX Armeekorps. As soon as a gap appeared in the German front, Gordov committed Volkhov's 5th Mechanized Corps at Koshelevo, 14km south of Terenino, and the mechanized brigades began to shove their way through the wrecked enemy battle groups in its path. In order to assist Gordov's attack, the 10th and 49th armies conducted probing attacks against the rest of Gruppe Harpe's front, preventing any transfer of units to reinforce the crumbling left flank.

At the same time, the 21st Army and 10th Guards Army attacked Kampfgruppe Vincenz's positions around Terenino station, which was only held by one infantry battalion and a *Pionier* unit. Schmidt immediately committed his meagre tactical reserves: two battalions from 35.Infanterie-Division and a company of assault guns (2./Sturmgeschütz-Abteilung 237). However, von Kluge would not allow the *Kampfgruppe* from 2.Panzer-Division to be committed yet, since Soviet armour had not yet broken through the German front. For about eight hours, Kampfgruppe Vincenz managed to contest the area around Terenino station before it was shattered into multiple fragments, which began falling back towards the Ugra River. Upon learning this, Heinrici ordered IX Armeekorps to make Yelnya defensible. Overall, it had been a good day for the Western Front, which had managed to advance 6–8km and created a gap between IX Armeekorps and Gruppe Harpe.

On the second day of the offensive, the 10th Guards Army mopped up those German elements that had not yet made it over the Ugra River and began boldly pushing up the railway line towards Yelnya. Von Kluge finally authorized the *Kampfgruppe* from 2.Panzer-Division to launch a counterattack, but it was not clear where this effort should be made: east to block the 10th Guards Army, or south to block the 5th Mechanized Corps? As it was, 2.Panzer-Division had very limited combat resources and could little more than conduct a mobile delay action, primarily with its armoured reconnaissance battalion. Heinrici provided some army-level Panzerjägers

Soviet officers examine captured German heavy rocket launchers. Several batteries of rocket launchers were dug in behind important German positions in the 4.Armee sector, in order to support counterattacks. However, these short-range weapons lacked mobility and some were abandoned when positions were hastily evacuated. (Courtesy of the Central Museum of the Armed Forces, Moscow via www. Stavka.org.uk)

and some more *Pionier* units, but these proved little more than speed bumps to the relentless Soviet advance. By late in the day, IX Armeekorps' right flank was near collapse and the 5th Mechanized Corps had achieved a breakthrough. Gordov's 33rd Army then committed the 6th Guards Cavalry Corps, to further increase the disintegration of the German front.

On 30 August, despite light rain, the Soviet offensive gathered momentum. What little remained of Kampfgruppe Vincenz and 35.Infanterie-Division was in full retreat. Supported by some fighter-bomber sorties, 2.Panzer-Division made some offensive jabs at the advancing Soviet units but could not stop them. After losing two PzKpfw IV medium tanks, the *Kampfgruppe* of 2.Panzer-Division withdrew to the south-west, with just 13 tanks and 787 combat troops left. At noon, Krylov's 21st Army committed Burdeyney's 2nd Guards Tank Corps, which effortlessly ploughed through the enemy wreckage in its path, advancing 20km in just a few hours. Simultaneously, Trubnikov's 10th Guards Army also made good progress, pushing back the right flank of 342.Infanterie-Division and advancing directly upon Yelnya with Stuchenko's 29th Guards Rifle Division and the 119th Tank Regiment in the lead. Luftwaffe reconnaissance observed 70 enemy tanks advancing up the railway line towards Yelnya and the Schlachtflieger were ordered to hit them. For once, Soviet ground troops enjoyed effective air cover while the Luftwaffe was unable to intervene; Yak-1M fighters from the Free French Normandie-Nieman Group shot down three Ju-87 Stukas over the Yelnya sector. By 1330hrs, Schmidt realized that Yelnya could not be held and requested permission from Heinrici to begin evacuating the city; approval arrived within minutes.

Since the right flank of IX Armeekorps had disintegrated, Schmidt was forced to extemporize some blocking units from whatever was available. Oberst der Reserve Friedrich Beyse, an artilleryman from the corps-level Arko 139, was given command of a motley collection of Flak troops and construction personnel and told to delay the enemy for

German artillery withdrawing. Most of the German division-level artillery was still horse-drawn, which made it difficult to withdraw under fire. Usually only the *Panzergrenadier-Divisionen* and *Heeresartillerie* units were provided with tracked prime movers. (From Nik Cornish@ Stavka.org.uk)

as long as possible. Beyse was told that reinforcements were on the way. Indeed, Heinrici transferred a battalion from 18.Panzergrenadier-Division (I./Panzergrenadier-Regiment 51) and von Kluge sent a single infantry battalion (I./Grenadier-Regiment 544) from 330.Infanterie-Division, but these units were off-loaded at Glinka, 20km north-west of Yelnya. The armoured train Panzer Zug 61 was also transferred to IX Armeekorps. A fresh formation, the 1.SS-Infanterie-Brigade (mot.), was en route to 4.Armee but would not arrive for another day. Beyse tried to block the main road south-east of Yelnya with elements of Flak-Regiment 35 but Burdeyney's tankers arrived before any 8.8cm Flak guns could be emplaced. By 1700hrs, Soviet infantry and tanks were attacking into Yelnya and Kampfgruppe Beyse put up only a brief rear-guard action before retreating into woods west of the city. During the night, 4.Armee was informed that Yelnya had been lost at 1900hrs on 20 August. From Yelnya, it was only 75km to Smolensk.

Further south, Gruppe Harpe was also under great pressure from the 33rd and 49th armies and was beginning to pull back towards Roslavl, which widened the gap between IX Armeekorps and Harpe's command. German situation maps showed only 'blocking detachments' in the gap between the two corps, but in reality these fragments were capable of nothing more than a fighting retreat. The presence of 5.Panzer-Division helped to prevent Gruppe Harpe's retreat from becoming a rout and rear-guards managed to inflict heavy losses on some of the pursuing Soviet troops. In Grishin's 49th Army, the 344th Rifle Division suffered 2,000 casualties in just three days of fighting – about one-third of its strength.

The sudden loss of Yelnya and the heavy losses suffered by Schmidt's IX Armeekorps caused Heinrici to order a partial withdrawal in the XXXIX Panzerkorps sector. Heinrici's intent was for Martinek's XXXIX Panzerkorps to refuse its right flank in order to conform with the retreat of Schmidt's IX Armeekorps, but this could necessitate the abandonment of the town of Dorogobuzh. Sokolovsky also saw the liberation of Yelnya as a decision

A British-made Valentine tank with a Red Army unit. The Valentine was moderately useful in the infantry support role, but its firepower was relatively limited. Note that the ride fender is missing and the left is mangled – the Russians tended to be very rough on their tanks. In the pursuit phase of *Suvorov*, the slower British tanks had difficulty maintaining contact with the enemy. (Author's collection)

point in the campaign and he now ordered Polenov's 5th Army – which had not joined in the initial attacks – to attack the left flank of Schmidt's XII Armeekorps. Polenov advanced with five rifle divisions and tank support against 252.Infanterie-Division, which was holding a 20km-wide front. Within just a few hours, Polenov's vanguard overran the German outpost line, which was only serving as rear-guards. The rest of 252.Infanterie-Division retreated westwards, just ahead of Polenov's 5th Army, which advanced 13km in a single day. Advance units reached the Yelnya–Dorogubuzh road near Artyushino before nightfall. Throughout 31 August, there was intense aerial combat over Dorogobuzh and Yelnya, in which the Normandie-Nieman Group claimed ten victories (four Fw-190, five Ju-87, one He-111) for the loss of two of their own fighters.

Given the rapid retreat of 252.Infanterie-Division and the threat of envelopment from the 5th Army, it was now pointless to mount a defence of Dorogobuzh. At noon on 30 August, XXXIX Panzerkorps ordered 337.Infanterie-Division and Gruppe Krägeloh to abandon the town and retreat west 20km to the Uzha-Stellung, behind a minor tributary of the Dnepr. By the time that 337.Infanterie-Division began to fall back, elements of the 5th Army were turning their right flank and it became a race to avoid being cut off. The 337.Infanterie-Division won the race, but only at the cost of abandoning a good deal of equipment, including a number of motor vehicles awaiting repair. No sooner had 337.Infanterie-Division reached the west bank of the Uzha, Soviet infantry was spotted crossing the 10m-wide river near Kalita (13km south-west of Dorogobuzh). Only a single German battalion (II./Grenadier-Regiment 688) was available in this sector, but it managed to counterattack and prevent the Soviets from gaining a firm bridgehead across the river.

On 1 September, soldiers of the 312th Rifle Division, 5th Army, entered the empty town of Dorogobuzh. Polenov was able to mount a hasty attack on the Uzha-Stellung at the same time, but more German counterattacks repulsed his river-crossing attempts for the time being. Gluzdovsky's 31st

German security troops conducting an anti-partisan operation in Russia, October 1943. Korück 559 was responsible for rear-area security in the Smolensk area, but lacked the resources to mount a successful counter-insurgency campaign. (Bundesarchiv, Bild 146-1993-066-23A, Foto: Dreyer)

Army also continued attacking and managed to push back 252.Infanterie-Division in some disarray. However, Martinek's XXXIX Panzerkorps was able to hold its position on the Uzha-Stellung and it had avoided serious damage. The northern end of the line was anchored east of Yartsevo by the stalwart 18.Panzergrenadier-Division. Intense air combat continued over the area, as both sides struggled to gain air superiority over the Dorogobuzh–Yelnya sectors. Leytenant Arseniy I. Morozov, a fighter pilot in the 49th Fighter Aviation Corps, distinguished himself in one such aerial skirmish west of Yelnya in which his regiment claimed eight victories.

The key sector was now the Yelnya–Smolensk axis, where the remnants of Schmidt's IX Armeekorps were not able to establish a continuous front. By 1 September, Heinrici was looking at a full-blown catastrophe. A sudden, violent thrust in this direction by Soviet armour could shatter 4.Armee's entire front and precipitate a rout. However, Sokolovsky's vanguard units were once again plagued by shortages of fuel, ammunition and transport to maintain offensive momentum. He still had about 300 operational tanks, but fuel and ammunition in front-line units was negligible. Leutnant Armin Scheiderbauer, 252.Infanterie-Division, noted that the advancing Soviets were recruiting local civilians to assist their logistical effort and were even using old men, women and children to roll fuel barrels westwards along roads. Whether this was true or not, the retreating Wehrmacht made a point of taking as many civilians with them as possible, in order to deny personnel resources to the enemy. Furthermore, Soviet losses were also debilitating and nine of Sokolovsky's attacking rifle divisions were reduced to 3,000 men or less.

Competition between Soviet front commanders also helped to rob momentum from Sokolovsky's advance. Popov's Bryansk Front had begun its own offensive against 9.Armee on 1 September, but was not making rapid progress. Popov requested troops from the Western Front to support his drive on Bryansk, which was approved by Stavka. Instead of pushing north-west towards Smolensk, Sokolovsky was told to redirect his 10th Army

Panzer Zug 61 was used primarily to protect Heeresgruppe Mitte's line of communications against partisans, but in mid-September 1943 it was pressed into front-line service in response to the Soviet breakthrough. The armoured train ended up conducting a successful rear-guard action at Dobromino, which delayed the Soviet advance to the Dnepr River. (Bundesarchiv, Bild 101I-639-4252-19A, Foto: Zwirner)

and part of his mobile forces southwards against Gruppe Harpe. Leytenant Dmitri Loza noted that the marshy terrain in this sector was poorly suited to the Matilda tank, with soft mud getting clogged up under the side skirts. Although this redirection helped to secure more terrain, Harpe simply traded space for time and withdrew southwards, so the benefit for Soviet operational objectives was negligible. In the interim, Heinrici placed the newly arrived 1.SS-Infanterie-Brigade to block the Yelnya–Smolensk axis while Schmidt's IX Armeekorps tried to reassemble its retreating fragments back into functional units. Von Kluge also agreed to release the rest of 330. Infanterie-Division to reinforce this sector and he ordered Model to transfer another division from 9.Armee, the 78.Sturm-Division. Oberst Heinz Fiebig, commander of 4.Armee's weapons-training school, was put in charge of organizing the arriving SS-Brigade and a regiment from 330.Infanterie-Division into a temporary command, which was designated Division Fiebig.

By 3 September, Heinrici had established a tenuous new front line, anchored by XXXIX Panzerkorps east of Yartsevo and Division Fiebig west of Yelnya. When 78.Sturm-Division arrived in the IX Armeekorps sector, Heinrici shifted 1.SS-Infanterie-Brigade to reinforce XXXIX Panzerkorps. Model transferred the schwere Panzer-Abteilung 505 to 4.Armee and a *Kampfgruppe* with five Tiger heavy tanks was attached to 20.Panzer-Division south-west of Yelnya. Although few in numbers, the Tigers easily picked off the small number of Soviet tanks still active at the front in this sector. Sokolovsky continued local attacks throughout the first week of September, but lacked the strength to break through even this modest German front line. Once again, Sokolovsky's offensive had prematurely culminated due to logistical shortages. Although his army had survived this second ordeal, Heinrici knew that it was only a short respite. He used the time wisely, ordering units to begin construction of new defensive lines. Behind the current HKL, dubbed the Hubertus-I-Stellung, Heinrici ordered construction of two further back-up positions: Hubertus II and Hubertus III. Leutnant Scheiderbauer was sent back with a construction detail from Grenadier-Regiment 7 and together with several *Bau-Bataillone* (construction battalions) from 4.Armee, they laboured furiously to dig new trench lines. Further back, the Organization Todt began work on the Panther-Stellung, east of Vitebsk and Orscha. However, 4.Armee had suffered another 15,000 casualties and most of its divisions were now burnt-out wrecks. Nor were any major reinforcements likely until later in the year, so it was unclear who would defend these new positions.

On 3 September, von Kluge flew to Hitler's headquarters in East Prussia, the Wolfsschanze, to discuss the deteriorating situation at the front. Generalfeldmarschall Erich von Manstein, commander of Heeresgruppe Süd, accompanied von Kluge and they jointly hoped to persuade him to either provide additional reinforcements from the Western Front or to authorize a withdrawal to avoid the next round of Soviet offensives. Von Manstein's forces had just lost Kharkov and were being repeatedly bludgeoned by the main weight of the Red Army. It was only a matter of time until Heeresgruppe Süd's front cracked, and if it retreated, Heeresgruppe Mitte would have to retreat as well. However, Hitler proved unwilling to reduce the level of forces sent to deal with the Allied invasion of mainland Italy, nor would he authorize any withdrawals on the Eastern Front unless absolutely necessary. Instead, he simply suggested that both commanders take troops from quiet sectors to replenish their losses – which had already been done. Von Kluge returned to Smolensk empty-handed. A few days later, von Kluge ordered the headquarters for Heeresgruppe Mitte shifted back to Orscha, but Heinrici's 4.Armee headquarters remained in Smolensk.

From Sokolovsky's point of view, the second phase of Operation *Suvorov* was far more fruitful than the first phase, but his operational decisions were still being shaped by his logistical shortcomings. Without stockpiles of fuel and ammunition, he could only afford to attack in short offensive pulses. He recognized that the German retreat had stopped and that it would require another offensive pulse to reach Smolensk. On 7 September, Stavka approved another temporary suspension of Operation *Suvorov*, with one week allowed for logistical replenishment.

THE THIRD ROUND, 14 SEPTEMBER– 2 OCTOBER 1943

By 9 September, Heinrici had three corps arrayed south, east and north of Smolensk. Schmidt's IX Armeekorps was defending a 40km front with five infantry divisions that had a total of only 22 battalions with 6,277 men. Bits and pieces of 13 more battalions were rebuilding in the rear. Martinek's XXXIX Panzerkorps was holding a 43km-wide front with two divisions, totalling 5,234 front-line troops. Völckers' XXVII Armeekorps held an 81km-wide sector with five divisions totalling about 10,000 troops. Expecting the main threat to develop from east of Dukhovshchina, Völckers positioned 25.Panzergrenadier-Division, augmented by 1.SS-Infanterie-Brigade (mot.) east of the city, with the remaining elements of 18.Panzer-Division in tactical reserve. Altogether, 4.Armee was expected to hold a 164km front with just 21,500 troops. Even by scraping up all the scattered fragments of units, Heinrici could not put 30,000 troops in the front line. The only consolation for Heinrici was that being so close to Smolensk greatly simplified his logistics, which meant that his remaining troops had more fuel and ammunition than their opponents. On Heinrici's right flank, Gruppe Harpe (including XII Armeekorps) was equally hard-pressed to hold Roslavl.

Third phase of Operation *Suvorov*, 13–15 September 1943

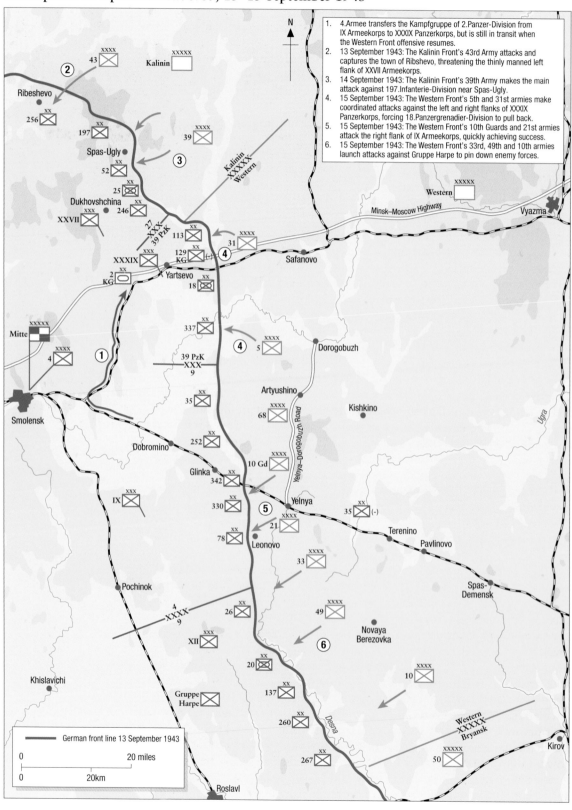

1. 4.Armee transfers the Kampfgruppe of 2.Panzer-Division from IX Armeekorps to XXXIX Panzerkorps, but is still in transit when the Western Front offensive resumes.
2. 13 September 1943: The Kalinin Front's 43rd Army attacks and captures the town of Ribshevo, threatening the thinly manned left flank of XXVII Armeekorps.
3. 14 September 1943: The Kalinin Front's 39th Army makes the main attack against 197.Infanterie-Division near Spas-Ugly.
4. 15 September 1943: The Western Front's 5th and 31st armies make coordinated attacks against the left and right flanks of XXXIX Panzerkorps, forcing 18.Panzergrenadier-Division to pull back.
5. 15 September 1943: The Western Front's 10th Guards and 21st armies attack the right flank of IX Armeekorps, quickly achieving success.
6. 15 September 1943: The Western Front's 33rd, 49th and 10th armies launch attacks against Gruppe Harpe to pin down enemy forces.

The Luftwaffe situation also changed markedly after the second round of Operation *Suvorov*. Von Greim was forced to commit the bulk of his remaining airpower to support Model's hard-pressed 9.Armee in the bitter fight to hold onto Bryansk (which was finally abandoned on 17 September). Some bomber units from Luftflotte 6 were also sent further back, to airfields at Orscha and Mogilev, because the airfields around Smolensk were under frequent air attack now. Consequently, Heinrici's 4.Armee had significantly less air support available by mid-September 1943, thereby losing one of the few advantages it had heretofore possessed.

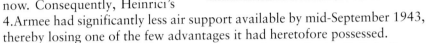

Soviet partisans preparing to blow up a section of railway line. By mid-1943, Soviet partisan units had become a serious thorn in Heeresgruppe Mitte's side by harassing its lines of communications. Although the VVS failed to mount an effective rail interdiction campaign in support of *Suvorov*, the partisans admirably filled this role. (Author's collection)

Eremenko decided to make some major changes in the Kalinin Front, beginning with removing Zygin from command of the 39th Army and replacing him with General-leytenant Nikolai E. Berzarin. Since Stavka was planning on transferring Oslikovsky's 3rd Guards Cavalry Corps to the Western Front, Eremenko recreated the Mobile Group of Kalinin Front under Polkovnik Ivan. F. Dremov in order to have an exploitation force. Eremenko also recognized that XXVII Armeekorps had strengthened the Barbarossa-Stellung north-east of Dukhovschchina with 1.SS-Infanterie-Brigade (mot.) and he decided to temporarily shift his main effort to Golubev's 43rd Army to throw Völckers off balance. On the morning of 13 September, the 91st Rifle Corps from the 43rd Army mounted a successful attack against the left flank of 256.Infanterie-Division, supported by over 100 sorties from 3rd Air Army. Heretofore this sector had not seen as much Soviet activity and it was not held in great strength, which enabled the 43rd Army to advance and capture the town of Bedenki. Völckers told 256.Infanterie-Division to clear up this local enemy success with its own resources, since he had nothing to spare.

Hoping that Völckers would commit at least some reserves to his left flank to counter the attack by the 43rd Army, Eremenko struck the centre of the enemy line near Spas-Ugly on the morning of 14 September. After a 20-minute artillery preparation, the 39th Army attacked 197.Infanterie-Division and 52.Infanterie-Division with four rifle divisions, which quickly smashed Grenadier-Regiment 163 and created a breach in the German front. The right flank of 197.Infanterie-Division was also penetrated. By 1000hrs, Eremenko committed both Dremov's mobile group and Tank Group Chuprova, which caused 52.Infanterie-Division to collapse across a wide area. Kampfgruppe Kopenhagen, the only surviving element of the division, was enveloped and routed. Virtually all the divisional artillery was lost in the sudden retreat. Supporting attacks by the 83rd Rifle Corps pinned down 25.Panzergrenadier-Division, but failed to achieve any success in this sector. Before long, Völckers was receiving reports that enemy vehicles were appearing well behind the front, in Beresnevo, Ponomari and Kuzmichino.

Soviet infantrymen attacking into a town. There was remarkably little urban combat during Operation *Suvorov* since the Germans usually evacuated large towns and cities once the outer defences became untenable. However, in a few places, like Yartsevo, there was a brief period of street fighting. In general, the Wehrmacht proved unwilling to conduct last-ditch fights for Soviet cities. (Courtesy of the Central Museum of the Armed Forces, Moscow via www. Stavka.org.uk)

He immediately committed part of the anaemic 18.Panzer-Division to counterattack at Filippovo and assist Gruppe Kopenhagen to retreat. Another mobile group from 18.Panzer-Division, little more than a few companies, went to clean up the situation at Ponomari and Kuzmichino. However, Völckers had nothing to deal with the Chuprova Group tanks in Beresnevo; he appealed to von Kluge, who sent him a single battalion from Sturm-Regiment 4.Armee. This battalion arrived by rail during the evening and was inserted to plug the wide gap south of Beresnevo.

On 15 September, the 39th Army expanded its penetration of the Barbarossa-Stellung and mopped up bypassed positions, but made little effort to immediately capitalize on its initial success. The 43rd Army also chewed away at the left flank of 256.Infanterie-Division, finally capturing the town of Ribshevo. Although the right flank of XXVII Armeekorps, anchored by 25.Panzergrenadier-Division, was still solid, the left flank was crumbling fast. Völckers could see that his front was breached in two places and that 197.Infanterie-Division was threatened with encirclement. Holding off as long as possible, in the afternoon Völckers finally ordered his corps to begin falling back towards the Hubertus-I-Stellung. As German front-line resistance faded, Soviet units began surging forward in pursuit. On the morning of 16 September, the 2nd Guards Rifle Corps and 84th Rifle Corps linked up at Klevtsi, 11km north of Dukhovshchina, but 197.Infanterie-Division had escaped the pincers.

During 16 September, Völckers tried to reorganize his battered units as they reached the Hubertus-I-Stellung, while his covering forces delayed the enemy. Hauptman Heinz Wersig, commander of Sturmgeschütz-Abteilung 190, formed part of the rear-guard north of Dukhovshchina, but his StuG III was knocked out by advancing Soviet tanks. It was evident that 52.Infanterie-Division and 197.Infanterie-Division were nearly combat-ineffective and that 256.Infanterie-Division was arriving piecemeal, which meant that there were not enough combat troops to form a continuous front line. Meanwhile, the 2nd Guards Rifle Corps and Dremov Mobile Group pushed south on the road to Dukhovshchina, brushing aside German rear-guards. Realizing that his remaining forces would be crushed if he tried to make a stand on the Hubertus-I-Stellung, Völckers ordered the evacuation of Dukhovshchina on the night of 16/17 September. The next day, the 17th Guards Rifle Division was the first unit to enter the city. After abandoning Dukhovshchina, the XXVII Armeekorps paused further south to regroup. The Germans claimed to have knocked out 200 tanks from the Kalinin Front in the brief offensive, which may have helped to slow Eremenko's pursuit. On the other hand, 52.Infanterie-Division was virtually destroyed and most of the remainder of

18.Panzer-Division was withdrawn, leaving only Kampfgruppe Lang as a mobile reserve.[7]

Meanwhile, 26km to the south-east, on the morning of 15 September Gluzdovsky's 31st Army attacked von Erdmannsdorff's 18.Panzergrenadier-Division positions 12km east of Yartsevo on the Minsk–Moscow Highway. Heinrici had massed his best available forces at this key location and reinforced 18.Panzergrenadier-Division with Sturmgeschütz-Abteilung 185 (19 operational StuG III), two battalions of *Heeresartillerie* and extra *Panzerjäger*. Rather than tackle the German strongpoint head on, Gluzdovsky weighted his initial attacks on his right flank, with the 36th Rifle Corps striking 113.Infanterie-Division. Once again, this fragile division gave ground when pressed. Simultaneously, Polenov's 5th Army – reduced to just three rifle divisions with no armour support – attacked 337.Infanterie-Division. Given that this division was holding a 26km-wide front, Polenov's troops were able to gain some ground and the Germans had no tactical reserves left to plug these penetrations. With the neighbouring divisions on both flanks falling back, von Erdmannsdorff was forced to retreat to the outskirts of Yartsevo to maintain a continuous front.

Most of the town of Yartsevo was on the eastern bank of the Vop and the 31st Army fought its way into the ruins, led by the 274th Rifle Division. Podpolkovnik Piotr Dodogorsky led his 961st Rifle Regiment in the street fighting in Yartsevo; he had been a platoon leader during the Battle of Smolensk in 1941 and was one of the new breed of veteran Soviet combat leaders. Eventually, 18.Panzergrenadier-Division retreated to the west side of the river, leaving most of the town in Soviet hands. Yartsevo had a pre-war population of 36,000, but only 4,000 civilians remained in the ruins. The loss of both Dukhovshchina and Yartsevo effectively opened the door to a rapid advance upon Smolensk. Upon hearing of the liberation of both towns, Stalin ordered twelve artillery salvoes fired in Moscow to commemorate the event and awarded honorific titles to the units involved.

With Heinrici suitably distracted by Eremenko's attack on the XXVII Armeekorps, Sokolovsky prepared to make his main effort with the 68th, 10th Guards, 21st and 33rd armies against Schmidt's IX Armeekorps' positions in the Hubertus-I-Stellung west of Yelnya. Schmidt was assigned to hold a 40km-wide front with five decimated divisions. The *Kampfgruppe* from 2.Panzer-Division was supposed to be the tactical reserve for this critical sector, but Heinrici had decided to transfer it to Martinek's XXXIX Panzerkorps to reinforce the losing battle at Yartsevo. Instead, Heinrici transferred Jäger-Bataillon 4 and a single *Pionier-Kompanie* to give Schmidt some kind of reserve. As it turned out, 2.Panzer-Division arrived too late to

A young German lieutenant on the Eastern Front, mid-1943. The Wehrmacht still had an edge in junior tactical leadership, but platoon leaders were now being killed off more quickly than they could be replaced. In some cases, German infantry platoons were being led by junior NCOs – the combat efficiency of the Wehrmacht was beginning to disintegrate. (Süddeutsche Zeitung Bild 00051920, Foto: Schürer)

7   Kampfgruppe Lang consisted of a single Panzergrenadier Kompanie, a Pionier Kompanie, two artillery batteries and a Panzerjäger detachment. The cadre from 18.Panzer-Division was used to form 18.Artillerie-Division.

DEFEAT OF XXVII ARMEEKORPS, 13–17 SEPTEMBER 1943

The main effort came from the Soviet 39th Army, which launched a major attack against the centre of XXVII Armeekorps' front and achieved major breakthroughs.

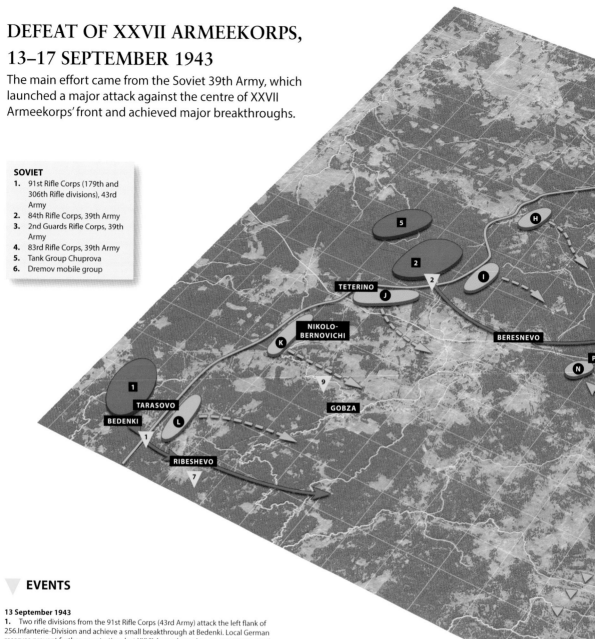

SOVIET
1. 91st Rifle Corps (179th and 306th Rifle divisions), 43rd Army
2. 84th Rifle Corps, 39th Army
3. 2nd Guards Rifle Corps, 39th Army
4. 83rd Rifle Corps, 39th Army
5. Tank Group Chuprova
6. Dremov mobile group

▼ EVENTS

13 September 1943
1. Two rifle divisions from the 91st Rifle Corps (43rd Army) attack the left flank of 256.Infanterie-Division and achieve a small breakthrough at Bedenki. Local German reserves prevent further penetration, but XXVII Armeekorps has no reserves to send to this sector.

14 September 1943
2. Dawn: The Soviet 39th Army launches a major attack against the centre of XXVII Armeekorps' front. The 84th Rifle Corps achieves a breakthrough near Teterino and tanks from Group Chuprova reach Beresnevo.

3. The 2nd Guards Rifle Corps achieves a major breakthrough south of Spas-Ugly, overwhelming Grenadier-Regiment 163.

4. 1000hrs: Eremenko commits the Dremov Mobile Group, which shatters the remainder of 52.Infanterie-Division and routs Gruppe Kopenhagen.

5. Morning: All attacks by the 83rd Rifle Corps are repulsed.

6. Afternoon: A counterattack by part of 18.Panzer-Division briefly stops the Soviet advance at Filippovo and assists the retreat of Gruppe Kopenhagen. Another part of the division retakes Kuzmichino.

7. The 91st Rifle Corps continues to envelop the left flank of 256.Infanterie-Division and captures Ribshevo.

8. Evening: A battalion from Sturm-Regiment AOK 4 arrives by rail and establishes a blocking position south of Beresnevo.

15 September 1943
9. The Soviets spend most of the day mopping up pockets of German resistance and widening their breakthrough zones. By evening, Völckers orders his corps to withdraw to the Hubertus-I-Stellung.

16 September 1943
10. Morning: The 2nd Guards Rifle Corps and 84th Rifle Corps link up at Klevtsi, but most of the Germans have avoided being encircled. Meanwhile, 91st Rifle Corps pursues 256.Infanterie-Division.

11. Evening: After a brief stand to regroup on the Hubertus-I-Stellung, XXVII Armeekorps evacuates Dukhovshchina.

17 September 1943
12. Morning: The 2nd Guards Rifle Corps and Dremov Mobile Group enter Dukhovshchina.

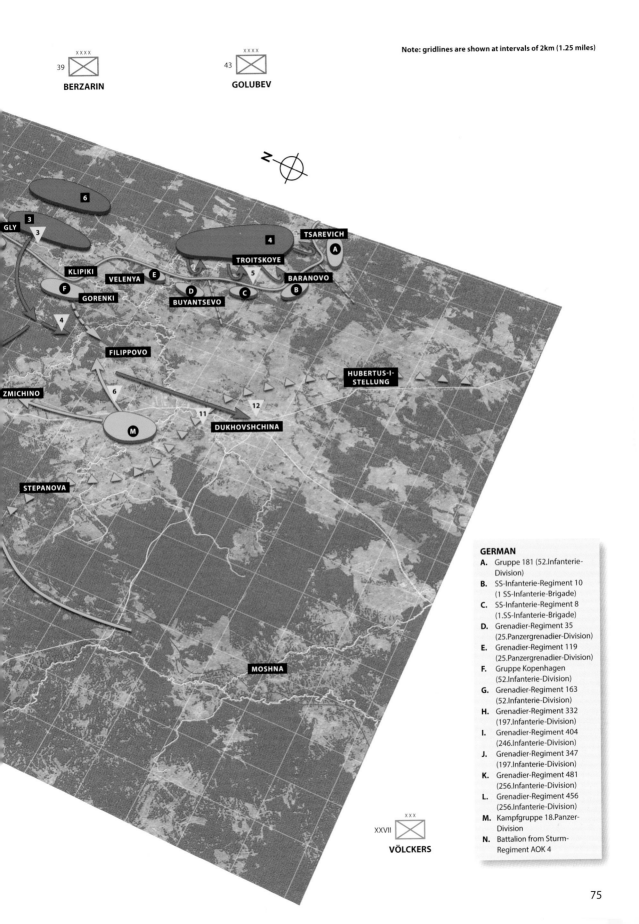

Note: gridlines are shown at intervals of 2km (1.25 miles)

39 XXXX ⊠
BERZARIN

43 XXXX ⊠
GOLUBEV

N

XXVII ⊠
VÖLCKERS

GERMAN
A. Gruppe 181 (52.Infanterie-Division)
B. SS-Infanterie-Regiment 10 (1 SS-Infanterie-Brigade)
C. SS-Infanterie-Regiment 8 (1.SS-Infanterie-Brigade)
D. Grenadier-Regiment 35 (25.Panzergrenadier-Division)
E. Grenadier-Regiment 119 (25.Panzergrenadier-Division)
F. Gruppe Kopenhagen (52.Infanterie-Division)
G. Grenadier-Regiment 163 (52.Infanterie-Division)
H. Grenadier-Regiment 332 (197.Infanterie-Division)
I. Grenadier-Regiment 404 (246.Infanterie-Division)
J. Grenadier-Regiment 347 (197.Infanterie-Division)
K. Grenadier-Regiment 481 (256.Infanterie-Division)
L. Grenadier-Regiment 456 (256.Infanterie-Division)
M. Kampfgruppe 18.Panzer-Division
N. Battalion from Sturm-Regiment AOK 4

Map labels: TSAREVICH, TROITSKOYE, BARANOVO, KLIPIKI, VELENYA, GORENKI, BUYANTSEVO, FILIPPOVO, ZMICHINO, DUKHOVSHCHINA, STEPANOVA, MOSHNA, HUBERTUS-I-STELLUNG, GLY

Soviet infantry, supported by a 45mm anti-tank gun, advance into a city. These well-equipped troops are likely from a Guards unit. (Courtesy of the Central Museum of the Armed Forces, Moscow via www. Stavka.org.uk)

save Yartsevo. During the night of 14/15 September, Sokolovsky's armies conducted aggressive probing all along Schmidt's front and pounded known German positions with artillery.

At 0545hrs on 15 September, the Soviets began a 90-minute artillery preparation against Schmidt's front-line positions, followed by intense bombing attacks. At 0715hrs, the artillery fire lifted and the ground attack began. Rather than pushing straight up the Smolensk–Yelnya railway line, Sokolovsky placed his main effort south of the tracks, near the town of Leonovo. General-mayor Aleksandr M. Ilin's 61st Rifle Corps from Krylov's 21st Army, supported by about 60 tanks, attacked 78.Sturm-Division between Ozerensk and Kukuyevo and punched a hole between II./Sturm-Regiment 215 and the I./Sturm-Regiment 14. Although an elite full-strength formation in Operation *Zitadelle* back in July, 78.Sturm-Division was now a battle-weary division and it buckled under the onslaught. Schmidt sent a few assault guns from Sturmgeschütz-Abteilung 237 to try to seal the breach, but the counterattack failed. At 1030hrs, Berzarin's 10th Guards Army struck the left flank of 330.Infanterie-Division with a mass of infantry and tanks, pushing back two battalions. All Schmidt could do was commit batteries from Flak-Regiment 35 to provide additional anti-armour support to 330. Infanterie-Division and request Luftwaffe bombing sorties. Both Krylov's 21st Army and Berzarin's 10th Guards Army continued attacking all morning and into the afternoon, creating additional small penetrations in several places. By 1320hrs, the right flank of 330.Infanterie-Division was also being pushed back. However, Sokolovsky did not achieve a penetration on the first day and the deepest the Soviets reached was only 3km, not the 13km claimed by Istomin. Nevertheless, the right flank of IX Armeekorps had been mauled, and at 1900hrs both 330.Infanterie-Division and 78.Sturm-Division were allowed to make minor withdrawals to straighten out their front lines.

On 16 September, Sokolovsky resumed his attacks at 0630hrs. Shock groups from five rifle divisions attacked 78.Sturm-Division and after six hours of fighting managed to advance 2km. At the same time, 15th Guards Rifle Corps from 10th Guards Army attacked the northern flank of 342.

A German Sdkfz 251/1 half-track pauses next to a concealed anti-tank gun. The 18. and 25.Panzergrenadier divisions, although quite depleted, proved to be the bedrock of 4.Armee's defence throughout the difficult days of August and September 1943. The ability of even small mechanized battle groups to rush to threatened sectors kept the front line from completely collapsing. (Süddeutsche Zeitung Bild 00024668, Foto: Scherl)

Infanterie-Division, just north of the railway line, but failed to make any substantive gains. Further north, the 68th Army continued probing attacks against 35.Infanterie-Division and 252.Infanterie-Division. Although Schmidt's front was still not broken after two days of heavy attacks, it was clear that the breaking point was near, and at 1600hrs on 16 September, Heinrici ordered IX Armeekorps to withdraw to the Hubertus-II-Stellung. During the night of 16/17 September, Schmidt began withdrawing to the west, using his assault guns and mobile Flak guns to provide the rear-guard. Meanwhile, the 10th and 49th armies had mounted powerful supporting attacks against Group Harpe, both to assist Sokolovsky's main effort and to assist the Bryansk Front's push towards Roslavl. Everywhere von Kluge looked, his forces were retreating.

Once the German withdrawal was detected, Sokolovsky committed all his mobile reserves to the fight on 17 September. The 2nd Guards Tank Corps and 5th Mechanized Corps pushed rapidly up the Smolensk–Yelnya railway line against the retreating 252.Infanterie-Division and inflicted considerable damage. One German rear-guard, including Panzer Zug 61, was isolated at Dobromino as the 2nd Guards Tank Corps pushed on past towards the Dnepr River. Amazingly, the armoured train and a group of rail *Pioniere*, led by Oberleutnant Peter Rang, managed to mount a successful breakout attack. However, both 35.Infanterie-Division and 252.Infanterie-Division were decimated in the withdrawal and unable to establish a new continuous front. When Leutnant Armin Scheiderbauer returned to his regiment after helping to construct the Hubertus-II-Stellung, he found that his company was reduced to just 35 men. Heinrici requested reinforcements to shore up the battered IX Armeekorps and von Kluge ordered Model to release the schwere Panzer-Abteilung 505, which was currently supporting the defence of Roslavl. On the other side, Sokolovsky intended to pursue the left wing of IX Armeekorps and approach Smolensk from the south with the 68th Army, 10th Guards Army and most of his armour. Meanwhile, the 21st and 33rd armies, including the 6th Guards Cavalry Corps, would pivot towards the south-west, with the objective of severing the Smolensk–Roslavl railway line near Pochinok.

By 18 September, Heinrici's 4.Armee was falling back to the Hubertus-II-Stellung with Sokolovsky's troops in pursuit. Gruppe Harpe on 4.Armee's right flank was also in retreat, under pressure from the Bryansk Front. On

Soviet sub-machine gunners advance through a wooded area under cover of smoke. Despite the huge amount of artillery and tank support, the Kalinin Front's breakthrough was ultimately achieved by aggressive, well-led rifle units that chewed their way through the German defences metre by metre. (Author's collection)

paper, the Hubertus-II and Hubertus-III *Stellungen* offered the potential to mount a last-ditch defence of Smolensk, but only very basic fieldworks actually existed. Priority for 4.Armee's construction units had been given to work on the Panther-Stellung, not intermediate lines. Furthermore, 4.Armee's front-line divisions were now too reduced to do anything but fight a delaying action. The 330.Infanterie-Division and 78.Sturm-Division had suffered heavy losses, including most of their anti-tank guns. Once the retreat began, the German army's reliance on horse transport proved a definite liability, since artillery units and support equipment could not outrun pursuing Soviet armoured units. The only bright spot was when the schwere Panzer-Abteilung 505 arrived by rail at Pochinok, and Heinrici ordered it to join IX Armeekorps as soon as possible. The next day, the Tigers reached the front and helped to cover the retreat of 330.Infanterie-Division. On the morning of 18 September, the Tigers of schwere Panzer-Abteilung 505 established a blocking position north-east of Strigino and managed to pick off 26 Soviet tanks for the loss of one Tiger, but this only briefly slowed the Soviet advance towards Pochinok. Although XXXIX Panzerkorps managed to use the Dnepr to temporarily stabilize its line, IX Armeekorps was a broken and retreating formation. The XXVII Armeekorps also continued to retreat, which exposed XXXIX Panzerkorps near Yartsevo to envelopment from the north. Thus, Heinrici had little choice but to order XXXIX Panzerkorps to pull back to the Hubertus-II-Stellung, as well.

With his army unable to stop the Soviet offensive pulses, Heinrici issued an order on 17 September to the commander of Smolensk to prepare the city for destruction. The order stipulated that Technische-Abteilung XI (mot.) had primary responsibility for preparing critical facilities for destruction, but all units would participate and form *Brand und Spengkommando* (Burning and Demolition) detachments to set fire to and destroy buildings when they left the city. The order to initiate the destruction would be issued once Red Army units approached the city.

Behind the German lines, Soviet partisan groups were ordered to make an all-out effort to sever enemy lines of communication known as Operation *Kontsert* (Concert), in order to prevent replacements from reaching Smolensk.

The liberation of Smolensk, 24–25 September 1943

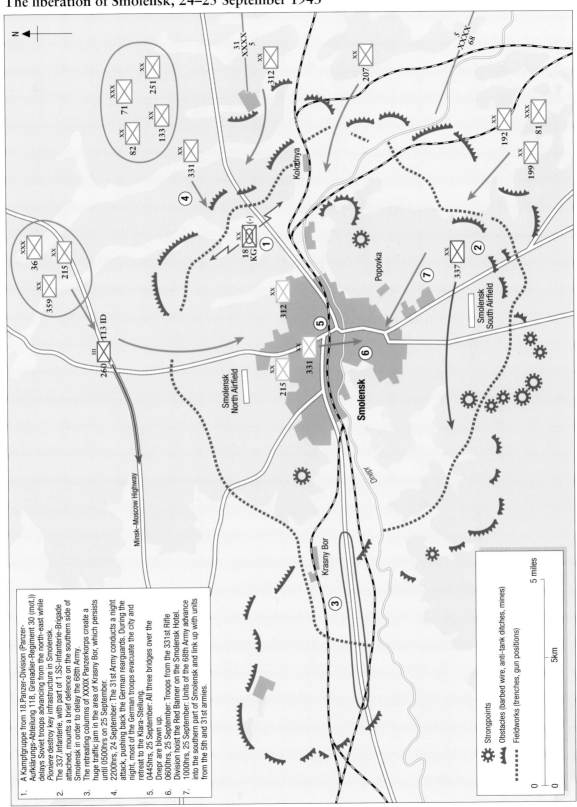

N

31 XXXX 5

312

XX 207

5 XXXX 68

XXX 71   251 XX

133 XX

82 XX

XX 331

192 XX   XXX 81

199 XX

Kolodnya

4

18 KG XX (-)

1

Popovka

2

XXX 36   XXX 215

359 XX

337 XX

7

Smolensk South Airfield

113 ID

260 XX III

312 XX

5

331 XX

6

215 XX

Smolensk North Airfield

Smolensk

Dnepr

Minsk–Moscow Highway

Krasny Bor

3

1. A Kampfgruppe from 18.Panzer-Division (Panzer-Aufklärungs-Abteilung 118, Grenadier-Regiment 30 (mot.)) delays Soviet troops advancing from the north-east while *Pioniere* destroy key infrastructure in Smolensk.
2. The 337.Infanterie, with part of 1.SS-Infanterie-Brigade attached, mounts a brief defence on the southern side of Smolensk in order to delay the 68th Army.
3. The retreating columns of XXXIX Panzerkorps create a huge traffic jam in the area of Krasny Bor, which persists until 0500hrs on 25 September.
4. 2200hrs, 24 September: The 31st Army conducts a night attack, pushing back the German rearguards. During the night, most of the German troops evacuate the city and retreat to the Klara-Stellung.
5. 0445hrs, 25 September: All three bridges over the Dnepr are blown up.
6. 0600hrs, 25 September: Troops from the 331st Rifle Division hoist the Red Banner on the Smolensk Hotel.
7. 1000hrs, 25 September: Units of the 68th Army advance into the southern part of Smolensk and link up with units from the 5th and 31st armies.

Strongpoints

Obstacles (barbed wire, anti-tank ditches, mines)

Fieldworks (trenches, gun positions)

5 miles

5km

0   0

A German 10.5cm lFH18 howitzer captured by the Kalinin Front in September 1943. During the retreat to the Hubertus-Stellung, 52.Infanterie-Division lost virtually all its artillery, including three batteries of 10.5cm and two batteries of 15cm howitzers. When the battlefield became fluid after a Soviet breakthrough, the German horse-drawn artillery units often could not escape in time. (Author's collection)

On the night of 19/20 September, Leutnant Helmut Schiebel was on a troop train heading east to join 18.Panzer-Division near Smolensk, when his journey was interrupted near Minsk. A large partisan unit had succeeded in blowing up a 10km-long stretch of track and attacked one of the line stations. Schiebel and all the troops on the train were formed into a lightly armed ad hoc unit to pursue the partisans, who of course were long gone. In order to discourage collaboration with the enemy, the partisans had also executed Soviet railway men who worked with the Germans, leaving the Germans short-handed on staff to operate railway stations. Due to this attack and others, it took Schiebel five days to travel roughly 200km. Operation *Kontsert* succeeded in disrupting German troop movements, which added further operational-level friction to Heinrici's conduct of the campaign.

After the liberation of Yartsevo, the 31st Army pushed steadily towards Smolensk along the Minsk–Moscow Highway, while the mass of the 10th Guards and 68th armies advanced from the south-west. The Dnepr River proved of little use to the retreating Germans, who were drawn inexorably towards Smolensk. Sokolovsky's forces were nearing exhaustion and supplies were low, but every Soviet soldier now sensed that a major victory was at hand; political commissars kept the troops fired up and moving, whether or not they had food or fuel. As it was, the converging Soviet armies had to pause for a few days outside Smolensk before making the final push. The 4.Armee was in poor condition itself, having lost a total of 577 machine guns, 133 mortars, 81 anti-tank guns and 39 artillery pieces in a week. German front-line morale was also fragile, as defeat followed defeat. German senior leadership was uninspired at this point, with little effort to rally

Soviet sappers building a pontoon bridge. As the Red Army advanced westwards, it became increasingly important to get tanks and artillery across water obstacles quickly, which made Soviet sapper units a valuable combat multiplier. (From Nik Cornish@ Stavka.org.uk)

A column of German soldiers marches past the Smolensk Hotel during the occupation. The hotel was used as a rest centre for German officers. On 25 September 1943, soldiers from the 331st Rifle Division stormed into the building and hoisted the Red Banner to signify the liberation of the city. (Author's collection)

fighting spirit. As Hitler had predicted, once he announced the creation of the Panther-Stellung, his front-line commanders only thought of retreating to this imagined sanctuary. Von Kluge intended to retreat to the Panther-Stellung as soon as possible, rather than try to defend Smolensk.

In order to put further pressure on 4.Armee, the Kalinin Front began attacking the right flank of 3.Panzerarmee near Demidov on 21 September; this thinly held sector was manned by only three *Jäger-Bataillone* (light infantry battalions). On the morning of 22 September, the Kalinin, Western and Bryansk fronts launched an all-out effort all along the front line from Demidov to Roslavl against the German positions in the Hubertus-III-Stellung. In some places, the Soviet attacks were repulsed, particularly if Tigers from schwere Panzer-Abteilung 505 or assault guns were available. Martinek's XXXIX Panzerkorps was even able to mount some spirited local counterattacks. However, the 68th Army achieved a clear breakthrough south-east of Smolensk, in the sector held by the remnants of 35.Infanterie-Division. North-west of Smolensk, the 43rd Army captured Demidov and began pushing 4.Armee's left flank back. By the morning of 23 September, it was clear that the Hubertus-III-Stellung could not be held, particularly with the gaps created by the retreat of Schmidt's IX Armeekorps. It was now time to save what could be saved. At 2030hrs on 23 September, Heinrici ordered 4.Armee to retreat to the Klara-Stellung, thereby signalling the evacuation of Smolensk.

Martinek's XXXIX Panzerkorps was assigned to conduct the rear-guard at Smolensk, while the rest of 4.Armee withdrew to the Klara-Stellung and *Pioniere* demolished key facilities in the city. A *Kampfgruppe* from 18.Panzergrenadier-Division and the remnants of 113.Infanterie-Division were positioned on the north-east approaches to the city, defending the Minsk–Moscow Highway, while 337.Infanterie-Division (with 1.SS-Infanterie-Brigade attached) defended the southern approaches. By this point, only two Tigers from schwere Panzer-Abteilung 505 were still operational and they were assigned to support 337.Infanterie-Division. Generalmajor Hans Oschmann, a signals officer, was put in charge of the rear-guard force inside the city, which consisted of a *Kampfgruppe* from 246.Infanterie-

REAR-GUARD ACTION, 0800HRS, 26 SEPTEMBER 1943 (PP. 82–83)

The bulk of the German forces evacuated Smolensk during the night of 24/25 September 1943, as elements of the Soviet 31st Army began to fight their way into the northern part of the city. Special German *Pionier* detachments demolished key facilities in the city, including all railway stations and bridges. Fires quickly spread throughout the city. Martinek's XXXIX Panzerkorps conducted the rear-guard action at Smolensk, pausing to fight only long enough to slow the Soviet pursuit. By 26 September, the Soviet 31st Army was beginning to advance west along the Minsk–Moscow Highway, but were slowed by German rear-guard actions.

Here, a Hornisse ('Hornet') tank destroyer from schwere Panzerjäger-Abteilung 655 (**1**) is deployed in a hull-down position on the side of the highway, with its commander scanning for signs of enemy movement. Armed with the deadly 8.8cm Pak

43 anti-tank gun, the Hornisse (later redesignated the 'Nashorn' in 1944) was capable of engaging and destroying Soviet T-34 medium tanks well outside their effective range. The idea here was to destroy the lead enemy vehicles then fall back to the next position, making the Soviet pursuit more cautious. Another anti-tank position would be just a few hundred metres back. At this point in the battle, the Germans were very short of infantry, so this Hornisse only has a single MG42 team (**2**) in direct support. The Red Army often used cavalry in the reconnaissance role because they could move cross-country quickly. The machine-gun team is keeping an eye out for cavalry scouts. Stragglers from the German retreat (**3**) pass by the rear-guard, including vehicles laden with wounded (**4**). In the distance, grey smoke still hangs over the smouldering pyre of Smolensk (**5**).

Division, security and *Pionier* units. The weather began to take a turn for the worse, with rain and thick cloud cover hindering air operations – although this likely benefitted the Germans more than the pursuing Red Army.

During the afternoon of 24 September, the Soviet armies converging on Smolensk mounted probing attacks against the covering forces of XXXIX Panzerkorps, but did not make a serious push until nightfall. Expecting a tough city fight in Smolensk, the Soviet army-level commanders held back most of their armour and relied upon their infantry to make the final push into the city. Gluzdovsky's 31st Army pressed against 18.Panzergrenadier-Division from the east, while Zhuralev's 68th Army pushed back 337. Infanterie-Division in the south. Although German resistance was weakening, it was sufficient to prevent any units from being cut off and providing adequate time for *Pioniere* in the city to conduct extensive demolitions. Within the city, there were three bridges over the Dnepr, which were primed for destruction as soon as German rear-guards retreated across them. At 2200hrs, Gluzdovsky mounted an all-out attack to breach the outer defences of the city. It was extremely unusual on the Eastern Front to launch a major night attack, but by this point Sokolovsky knew that 4.Armee was not likely to fight for Smolensk and he wanted the city secured before it was completely destroyed. The 18.Panzergrenadier-Division fell back through the city and a huge traffic jam occurred in the Krasny Bor area, which reduced movement to a speed of just 4km/h. Gromov's 1st Air Army should have committed the Pe-2 bombers of 2nd Bomber Aviation Corps to interdict the roads leading west from Smolensk – inflicting great slaughter on the packed retreating columns – but the VVS failed to grasp this golden opportunity. At 0446hrs on 25 September, German *Pioniere* blew up all three bridges over the Dnepr.

The 31st Army's attack into the northern part of Smolensk was led by General-mayor Sergei I. Iovlev's 215th Rifle Division, followed by the 133rd and 331st Rifle divisions. Iovlev was not only an NKVD officer, but he had served with a partisan group near Smolensk when his unit had been overrun in 1941. Meanwhile, elements of the 68th Army approached the southern side of the city, pushing back 337.Infanterie-Division. Rather than defend the city, the German rear-guards fell back, until only small detachments from 18.Panzergrenadier-Division were still in the city. Soviet troops advancing into the city could hear explosions as the train stations, power plant and water works were blown up. Contrary to Soviet accounts, German records indicate that there was no major street fighting inside Smolensk – the German troops retreated westwards as Soviet troops entered the wrecked city. Indeed, 18.Panzergrenadier-Division suffered fewer than 200 casualties in the delay actions around Smolensk.

By 0600hrs on 25 September, Soviet troops had occupied large parts of Smolensk and an advance guard battalion from the 331st Rifle Division, led by Kapitan Prokofy F. Klepach, had even crossed the Dnepr. Once across the river, Kapitan Klepach hoisted the Red Banner on the Smolensk Hotel, marking the liberation. Four hours later, units from the 68th Army entered the city from the south. Soviet generals were distressed to find that the Germans had done a very thorough job of demolishing Smolensk, with approximately 85 per cent of all buildings damaged or destroyed. Indeed, much of the city was still burning. On the same day that Smolensk was liberated, Gruppe Harpe abandoned Roslavl to the 10th Army.

AFTERMATH

During the immediate aftermath of the loss of Smolensk, Heinrici's 4.Armee made a brief stand on the Klara-Stellung before falling back to the Dora-Stellung on 26/27 September. The Soviet pursuit was sometimes aggressive, but the vanguard units were clearly exhausted and short on fuel. German units were also exhausted; Leutnant Armin Scheiderbauer recalled that during the retreat, German troops rarely got more than two hours sleep per night and they were constantly being told to keep falling back to stay ahead of the pursuers. By this point, Scheiderbauer's company had been reduced to just 15 men and one MG42 machine gun. The days were still warm, but the nights were now cold and often rainy, making for a dismal retreat. Soviet forces became rather tangled up in and around the ruins of Smolensk, forcing Eremenko and Sokolovsky to establish new boundaries between their fronts and armies. Battle-weary formations like the 10th Guards Army and the 21st Army were pulled out of the line to regroup. The onus of the pursuit along the Minsk–Moscow Highway fell on the 5th and 68th armies, while the 33rd Army pushed towards Mogilev.

Elements of 4.Armee began to occupy the Panther-Stellung on 29 September, and by 2 October the retreat was called off. Altogether, Heinrici had only five real divisions left with a total combat strength of 10,120 troops

Once it was clear that the city would be lost, the Germans initiated a systematic effort to destroy anything of value in Smolensk. The urban heart of the city was devastated by fire and demolition, leaving the remaining population without electricity, water or shelter for the coming winter. The utter destruction of Smolensk reduced the moment of liberation to a hollow triumph. (From Nik Cornish@ Stavka.org.uk)

Retreat to the Panther-Stellung, 20 September–2 October 1943

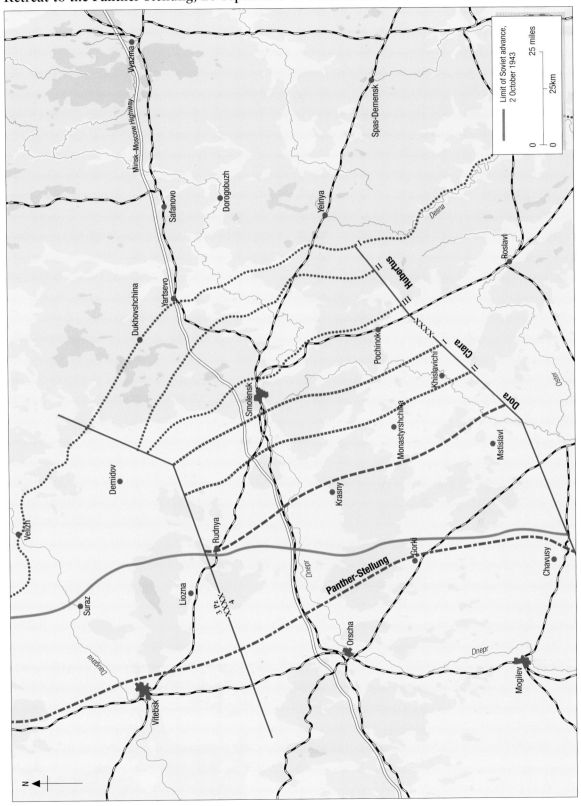

Vyazma

Minsk–Moscow Highway

Spas-Demensk

Safanovo

Dorogobuzh

Yelnya

Desna

Dukhovshchina

Yartsevo

Roslavl

Hubertus

Pochinok

Clara

Khislavichi

Oster

Smolensk

Demidov

Monastyrshchina

Mstislavl

Dora

Velizh

Krasny

Rudnya

Suraz

Liozna

Dnepr

Gorki

Chavusy

Panther-Stellung

XXXX
3 Pz
4

Daugava

Orscha

Dnepr

Vitebsk

Mogilev

Limit of Soviet advance,
2 October 1943

25 miles

25km

N

German demolitions in Smolensk, near the main train station. These 'scorched earth' tactics did not hinder the Soviet pursuit, although they did make the Red Army's logistic problems more acute – which contributed to the Western Front's failure to finish off 4.Armee in 1943. (Süddeutsche Zeitung Photo, 00398657, Foto: Scherl)

to defend a 133km-wide front. The 4.Armee's remaining armoured strength consisted of 16 Hornisse tank destroyers, 30 StuG III assault guns and nine medium tanks. Martinek's XXXIX Panzerkorps still had some residual combat power left, but both IX Armeekorps and XXVII Armeekorps were burnt-out wrecks. Too many of 4.Armee's infantry divisions had been reduced to brigade-sized *Kampfgruppen*; one of the worst hit, 52.Infanterie-Division, had been reduced to just three small infantry battalions (totalling 761 infantrymen) and 21 artillery pieces. The 113. Infanterie-Division had been gutted and its ranks were now filled with troops from several rear-area security battalions. The 35.Infanterie-Division and 330.Infanterie-Division and 18.Panzer-Division had been essentially destroyed. The OKH managed to send 4.Armee 5,000 replacements, along with the promise that 5,700 more would soon be on the way, but Heinrici had very few troops to hold the Panther-Stellung.

Stavka was eager for Sokolovsky to 'bounce' the Panther-Stellung before the Germans could create a firm defensive line, and ordered him to push on to Orscha. In Moscow, the liberation of Smolensk gave the impression that Heeresgruppe Mitte was routed and that Soviet forces might be able to reach the Lithuanian border before the onset of winter. Eremenko was ordered to advance to capture Vitebsk by 9–10 October, thereby assisting the advance of the Western Front towards Orscha. Stavka's orders were unrealistic given the poor condition of both the Western and Kalinin fronts, which were not even allowed time to repair damaged bridges or restock supplies. Eremenko's forces, led by the 5th Guards Rifle Corps and Dremov's mobile group, managed to storm the town of Rudnya on 29 September, but thereafter the German use of fortified towns reduced the advance to a crawl. It took two full days of heavy fighting to clear the Germans out of the next town, Liozna. The time bought by delaying Eremenko's advance enabled 3.Panzerarmee to establish a viable defence east of Vitebsk, which stopped the Kalinin Front's advance.

Meanwhile, Sokolovsky ordered the 5th and 31st armies to switch from pursuit to attack and destroy the German blocking forces along the Minsk–Moscow Highway and then capture Orscha. The 5th Army attacked XXVII Armeekorps on 3 October and managed to gain some ground before running out of steam. The German defence bent, but did not break – which was something of a miracle. At this point, Sokolovsky called an end to Operation *Suvorov*, which had accomplished its objectives. Local attacks continued to probe the German defences for another week, but the Western Front's grand offensive had run its course. Ignoring the state of front-line troops, Stavka kept issuing directives to Sokolovsky to mount a new offensive to breach the Panther-Stellung, but the Western Front was too depleted itself to make a serious effort. Instead, the Western Front's attacks in October and November

1943 degenerated into a stumbling fight between two exhausted opponents. By November, the OKH finally began providing adequate reinforcements to rebuild 4.Armee and the front stabilized for the winter.

As the Red Army advanced past the wreckage of Smolensk, the NKVD moved in to assess the situation. The postscript to liberation was revenge against those held to be responsible. In April 1943, the Presidium of the Supreme Soviet had issued the secret Decree No. 39 that stipulated prosecution for both German war criminals and Soviet citizens convicted of collaboration with the enemy occupation forces. In Smolensk, the NKVD began sifting through the population to identify alleged collaborators. During the autumn of 1945, Soviet tribunals in Smolensk convicted large numbers of collaborators and some were singled out for public execution. Having dealt with domestic enemies, the Soviet Union turned to deal with enemy war criminals by establishing special military tribunals in a number of cities, including Smolensk. Ironically, no senior German officers were indicted, not even the former head of the Gestapo in Smolensk. Instead, seven German enlisted soldiers, mostly from Sicherungs-Bataillon 335, were found guilty of war crimes against Soviet civilians in the Smolensk region and they were duly executed by hanging in Zadneprovskaya Square on 20 December 1945.

AN ASSESSMENT

The Western and Kalinin fronts had achieved a great victory in Operation *Suvorov*, by liberating Smolensk and pushing 4.Armee back over 200km. However, the offensive had sputtered along for 57 days in a frustrating start–stop fashion due to persistent shortages of fuel and ammunition. Nor could there be any victory parade for the cameras in Smolensk, since the city was a smouldering pile of rubble. Altogether, the Western and Kalinin fronts committed 1.2 million troops to Operation *Suvorov* and suffered a

As German troops pull out of Smolensk, small detachments of *Pioniere* prepare to lay mines to delay the enemy pursuit. The Waffen-SS soldiers on the vehicle may be from 1.SS-Infanterie-Brigade, which was part of the rear-guard. (From Nik Cornish@ Stavka.org.uk)

Before evacuating Smolensk, German security troops executed a numbers of Soviet prisoners, including both captured Red Army soldiers and local civilians accused of aiding the partisans. This kind of war crime only incited the Red Army to inflict the same kind of savagery on German civilians when they reached the Reich in 1945. (From the fonds of the RGAKFD, Krasnogorsk via www.Stavka.org.uk)

total of 451,466 casualties in the offensive, including 107,645 dead or missing. Sokolovsky lost 40 per cent of his original troop strength during the offensive – debilitating even by Red Army standards. Soviet material losses were also heavy during Operation *Suvorov*, including 863 tanks and over 300 aircraft. It would take months to restore the Western Front to a reasonable level of combat effectiveness, particularly given the wastage caused by the pointless fighting in October and November 1943. Although the Western Front had achieved its objectives, there was great dissatisfaction in the Kremlin about the uneven level of performance demonstrated during the operation. After *Suvorov*, there was a quiet purge of the Western Front, with Ilnitsky (intelligence), Kamera (artillery) and Gordov (33rd Army) relieved of command. Trubnikov had already been relieved of command of the 10th Guards Army before the end of *Suvorov*. Other senior officers in the Western Front were threatened with relief – which was probably far from the congratulatory tone that most were expecting after a major victory.

Aside from logistic problems, the operational-level methods used by the Western and Kalinin fronts at the start of *Suvorov* were inadequate, particularly in terms of *maskirovka* and air–ground coordination. The inability of the VVS to prevent Luftflotte 6 from interfering with Soviet ground deployments was just as much a hindrance as Soviet partisans were a hindrance to German troop movements. Tactically, the initial attacks on German fortified positions lacked cunning and simply shoved men, equipment and firepower forward without proper coordination. However, over the course of Operation *Suvorov*, the Red Army units improved considerably in their ability to accomplish missions, even though they were substantially reduced by casualties. By the third offensive pulse, Red Army units were able to engage German units on far more equitable terms, albeit still at the cost of excessive casualties.

From the German point of view, there was relatively little that either von Kluge or Heinrici could have done to alter the outcome, given their limited resources. Von Kluge took from Model's 9.Armee to help buttress Heinrici's 4.Armee, but ironically both armies suffered simultaneous defeats. In strategic terms, Hitler's extreme reaction to the Allied invasion of Italy caused him to divert Germany's limited pool of reinforcements at a critical moment after the defeat at Kursk. Valuable units, such as 16.Panzer-Division and 26.Panzer-Division, were sent to counterattack the Salerno landings instead of going to reinforce the crumbling Eastern Front. Other capable units, such as 1.Panzer-Division, were wasted guarding tertiary regions like Greece. It was not until November that Hitler finally allowed substantial reinforcements to be sent to mount counterattacks on the Eastern Front, by which point the situation was beyond retrieval. If the OKH had been able to introduce even two fresh mobile divisions to reinforce 4.Armee by late August, von Kluge might have been able to salvage more from this situation and limit the gains achieved by Operation *Suvorov*. As it was, the arrival of 25.Panzergrenadier-Division and 1.SS-Infanterie-Brigade proved to be

serious obstacles in the later phase of the Soviet offensive. Ultimately, Hitler's mismanagement of strategic priorities and resources were the proximate cause for the multiple German defeats suffered on the Eastern Front between July and September 1943.

Although Operation *Bagration* – the Soviet offensive against Heeresgruppe Mitte in June 1944 – has often been referred to as 'the destruction of Army Group Centre', the process of destruction actually began with Operation *Suvorov*. During August and September 1943, 4.Armee suffered over 54,000 casualties, including 14,454 dead or missing. The 4.Armee was forced to disband a number of battered divisions after the Smolensk campaign, including the 113, 268 and 330. *Infanterie-Divisionen*, while none of its remaining 'divisions' were, in fact, divisions. For example, 35.Infanterie-Division suffered over 3,600 casualties during *Suvorov*, which was more than its entire starting combat strength. By the time that these burnt-out divisions reached the Panther-Stellung, their ranks were made up of various odds and ends, mostly from rear-echelon personnel – a far cry from the victorious Wehrmacht of 1940–41. Equipment losses were also crippling, particularly in terms of artillery and anti-tank weapons, which further reduced the defensive capability of the remaining units. In the air, Luftflotte 6 lost over 100 aircraft, mostly fighters, trying to fend off the Western Front offensive. While the Luftwaffe still enjoyed a 3:1 kill ratio or better against the VVS, its days of superiority were gone and it could only occasionally influence events on the ground. Operation *Suvorov* was one of a series of Soviet offensives following the Battle of Kursk, which demonstrated that the Wehrmacht was no longer capable of stopping the relentless westward advance of the Red Army and that the Third Reich was doomed.

The Soviets conducted war crimes trials in Smolensk in late 1945, which resulted in the execution of a number of alleged civilian collaborators, as well as seven German soldiers. Virtually the entire population of Smolensk was ordered to witness these public hangings – obviously intended to demonstrate the cost of lapses in loyalty to the state. (From the fonds of the RGAKFD, Krasnogorsk via www. Stavka.org.uk)

THE BATTLEFIELD TODAY

As far as World War II battlefield tourism goes, Smolensk is off the beaten path and visitors would have to display some level of ingenuity to see much beyond bland Soviet-era memorials. Even though Smolensk currently has a population of over 326,000, it does not have an international airport and the nearest is over 200 miles to the east in Moscow. In order to get to Smolensk from a Western country, it would be necessary to fly into Moscow and then take the train from Belorussky railway station; four trains leave daily and the journey takes 4–5 hours. Smolensk has plenty of inexpensive hotels, making it a good location for a base of operations in the region and there are car rental services, as well. Furthermore, some tour and guide services are available in the Smolensk region, but these tend to focus on cultural heritage sites rather than World War II battlefields. For those seeking to visit the actual terrain where key actions in Operation *Suvorov* occurred, it is recommended to enlist the services of a private guide.

There is much to see in Smolensk itself, both in terms of general history, Napoleonic-era history and World War II. The 'Smolensk Region in Days of World War II 1941–1945' Museum located near Blon'ye Park is actually an eclectic mix of World War II equipment and some items from the Cold War era, like a MiG-23 fighter. This museum does have some interesting displays on the partisan movement as well as a full-size diorama of a Red Army machine-gun bunker. There are also a number of monuments in the city to heroes of the war, such as Mikhail Egorov, who raised the flag over the Reichstag in 1945. The remains of the Smolensk Kremlin (Fortress) in the south-east corner of the city are also an interesting attraction, with displays inside covering everything from Medieval-era warfare to 18th-century artillery. However, it should be pointed out that the bulk of the city was destroyed by the Germans in 1943 and there is relatively little on display that explains the actual liberation of the city, beyond a small memorial complex. Like most Russian war memorials, these sites are intended to honour the fallen, not enlighten visitors about the course of the campaign.

A memorial to the heroic Soviet troops who liberated Smolensk in September 1943. There are a number of other World War II-era monuments located in Smolensk, including several devoted to specific individuals. (Author's collection)

In order to actually see some of the terrain fought over in 1943, one would need to travel to Spas-Demensk and the smaller towns where more specific memorials are located. In August 2016, the township of Spas-Demensk opened the memorial complex 'Gnezdilovskaya Hill' (Гнездиловская Высота), which includes the much fought-over Hill 233.3. Over 4,000 Soviet soldiers are buried at the memorial complex and search teams continue to exhume remains and rusted equipment. Other towns such as Yartsevo, Yelnya and Dukhovshchina also have small military-related museums or memorials, often with long lists of casualties alongside. There are also monuments to partisan heroes. A good number of the villages that existed in 1943 do not exist anymore and even their locations can only be guessed. Most of the German positions reside in areas that are still heavily wooded and marshy, making access difficult. Aside from a few captured weapons in local museums, the German presence in the region has also been completely excised, but some fieldworks are still visible in remote areas.

Oddly, one of the more popular World War II-related tourist sites in the region is the house where Stalin remained overnight when conferring with Eremenko and Sokolovsky; this site, complete with a prominent bust, has been polished up as if Stalin might arrive at any moment to inspect it. Like many battlefields in Russia, the primary historical emphasis has been placed upon promoting a nationalist agenda for the consumption of Russian citizens, not illuminating military history details for inquisitive foreigners.

ABOVE LEFT A memorial atop Hill 233.3 ('Gnezdilovskaya Hill') near Gnezdilovo commemorates the sacrifices of the Western Front armies in August 1943, which led to the liberation of Spas-Demensk. In the background, there are panels that list approximately 4,000 fatalities suffered around this one small area. (Author's collection)

ABOVE RIGHT Exhumation of 1943-era casualties continues in the Gnezdilovo area, as it does across other parts of western Russia. Thousands of soldiers went missing in forests and marshes. These four dead soldiers will be interred with their fellows in the memorial complex. It is interesting that the Red Army, which had no chaplains in 1943, is now having the burial of its casualties attended by Russian Orthodox priests, indicating the mixture of religion and nationalism in the new Russia. (Author's collection)

FURTHER READING

Primary sources

This work was heavily based on original research from captured German reports held by the National Archives and Records Administration (NARA) in College Park, MD:

4.Armee (Ia, Ic, O. Qu.) from January–June 1943: T312, Rolls 216, 217, 218, 219

IX Armeekorps (Ia, KTB and Lagenkarten): Rolls 425–426

XXVII Armeekorps (Ia. KTB): T-314, Rolls 780–781. 'Die Abwehrschlachten des XXVII Armeekorps' on Roll 782.

XXXIX Armeekorps (Ia KTB, Ic): T314, Rolls 949–950

18.Panzergrenadier-Division (Ia, KTB): T315, Roll 701

56.Infanterie-Division (Ia): T-314, Rolls 975–976

113.Infanterie-Division (Ia, Ic): T-315, Roll 1293

260.Infanterie-Division: T-315, Roll 1826

268.Infanterie-Division (Ia, Lagenkarten und K.T.B.): T-315, Roll 1855

Secondary sources

Altukhov, P. K. et al, *Nezabyvayemyye dorogi. Boyevoy put' 10-y gvardeyskoy armii* (*Unforgettable Roads: Combat Route of the 10th Guards Army*) (Moscow: Military Publishing, 1974)

Cohen, Laurie R., *Smolensk Under the Nazis: Everyday Life in Occupied Russia* (Rochester, NY: University of Rochester Press, 2013)

Eremenko, Andrei, *Gody vozmezdiya. Boyevymi dorogami ot Kerchi do Pragi* (*Years of Retribution. Battle Roads from Kerch to Prague*) (Moscow: AST, 2009)

Fitisov, A. I. (ed.), *Khronika Osvobozhdeniya Spas-Demenskogo Rayona v Avguste 1943 goda* (*Chronicle of Liberation of Spas-Demensk District in August 1943*) (Moscow: Nauka, 2013)

Glantz, David M., *Battle for Belorussia: The Red Army's Forgotten Campaign of October 1943 – April 1944* (Lawrence, KS: University of Kansas Press, 2016)

Istomin, Vasily P., *Smolenskaya nastupatel'naya operatsiya 1943* (*Smolensk Offensive Operation 1943*) (Moscow: Military Publishing House, 1975)

Loza, Dmitry F., *Fighting for the Soviet Motherland: Recollections from the Eastern Front* (Lincoln, NE: University of Nebraska Press, 1998)

Scheiderbauer, Armin, *Adventures in My Youth: A German Soldier on the Eastern Front 1941–45* (Solihull, UK: Helion & Co. Ltd., 2010)

Scherzer, Veit, *113.Infanterie-Division, Kiew – Charkow – Stalingrad* (Jena: Scherzers-Militaer-Verlag Ranis, 2007)

GLOSSARY

Armeeoberkommando (AOK)	German Army Command
Artillerii Dal'nego Deystviya (ADD)	Soviet Long-Range Artillery Group
Bombardirovochnaya Aviatsionnaya Diviziya (BAD)	Soviet Bomber Aviation Division
Bombardirovochnaya Aviatsionnyi Korpus (BAK)	Soviet Bomber Aviation Corps
Field Ersatz-Bataillon (FEB)	German Field Replacement Battalion
Gvardeyskaya Armiya (GA)	Soviet Guards Army
Gvardeyskaya Artilleriyskaya Diviziya	Soviet Guards Artillery Division (GAD)
Gvardeyskaya Isrebitel'naya Aviatsionnaya Diviziya (GIAD)	Soviet Guards Fighter Aviation Division
Gvardeiskyi Isrebitelnyi Aviatsionnyi Polk (GIAP)	Soviet Guards Fighter Aviation Regiment
Gvardeiskyi Kavaleriyskiy Korpus	Soviet Guards Cavalry Corps (GCC)
Gvardeiskyi Shturmovoy Aviatsionnyi Polk (GShAP)	Soviet Guards Ground Attack Aviation Regiment
Gvardeiskyi Strelkovyi Korpus	Soviet Guards Rifle Corps (GRC)
Gvardeyskaya Strelkovaya Diviziya	Soviet Guards Rifle Division (GRD)
Gvardeyskaya Tankovaya Armiya (GTA)	Soviet Guards Tank Army
Hauptkampflinie (HKL)	German Main Line of Resistance
Heeresgruppe Mitte	German Army Group Centre
Isrebitel'naya Aviatsionnaya Diviziya (IAD)	Soviet Fighter Aviation Division
Isrebitelnyi Aviatsionnyi Korpus (IAK)	Soviet Fighter Aviation Corps
Jagdgeschwader	German fighter wing
Kampfgruppe	German ad hoc combined-arms combat formation
maskirovka	Soviet deception operations
Narodnyy Komissariat Vnutrennikh Del (NKVD)	Soviet People's Commissariat of Internal Affairs – the interior ministry of the Soviet Union
Oberkommando des Heeres (OKH)	German High Command
Ostheer	German Army in the East
Panzer-Divisionen	German Panzer divisions
PzKpfw	Panzerkampfwagen – German armoured vehicle
Rezerv Verhovnogo Glavnokomandovanija (RVGK)	Soviet Stavka Reserve
schwere Panzer-Abteilung	German Heavy Tank Battalion
Smeshannyi Aviatsionnyi Korpus (SAK)	Soviet Composite Aviation Corps
Shturmovoy Aviatsionnyi Diviziya (ShAD)	Soviet Ground Attack Aviation Division
Shturmovoy Aviatsionnyi Korpus (ShAK)	Soviet Ground Attack Aviation Corps
Stavka	Soviet High Command
StuG	Sturmgeschütz – German assault gun
Stützpunkte	German strongpoints
Voyenno-Vozdushnye Sily (VVS)	Soviet Air Force
Vozdushnaya Armiya	Soviet Air Army
Zapadnyy Front	Soviet Western Front

INDEX

Note: page numbers in bold refer to illustrations and captions and plates.